Building New Bridges

*Embracing the Hopes and Dreams
of Today*

By Jenna Kandyce Linch

**Building New Bridges
Embracing the Hopes and Dreams of
Today**

Copyright © 2009 by Jenna Kandyce Linch

No part of this book may be used or reproduced by any means, graphic, electronic, or mechanical, including photocopying, recording, taping or by any information storage retrieval system without the written permission of the publisher except in the case of brief quotations embodied in critical articles and reviews.

All Rights Reserved

ISBN 978-0-578-03439-3

Dedication

To all the underdogs in the world who have always been told they won't succeed in life, this book is for you. As underdogs, we're never expected to make it very far, yet here we are, still standing strong in life despite the odds that were against us. Never underestimate the underdogs in life for they are the ones who often take the world by surprise. Never stop believing in your dreams or yourself! When people tell you that you can't do something, remind yourself of how far you've made it all ready and keep holding onto those goals and dreams that will help guide you to where you want to be in life.

Introduction

This is yet another chapter in my own personal life as I continue to write the pages that are waiting to be filled, marking a new beginning and a new, improved sequel. As I wrote this volume of poetry, I was taken back to the early stages of my journey when I wasn't even sure where I would end up in life. Back then, I thought I had everything planned out all ready on how I wanted it to turn out, but life has a way of changing on us and as I found out, sometimes you may start out traveling on one road only to discover you're on an entirely different path all together. Looking back on my past reminds me of the struggles, hardships, and obstacles I had to overcome to be able to stand here today and be able to share the gift of hope and encouragement with others who are facing their own battles and challenges in their lives.

Dreams are so important in life because they give us something to hold onto and to believe in. I remember growing up I had so many different dreams of what I wanted to be when I got older. Unfortunately I grew up in a home where my parents did not believe in any of my dreams or goals and tried to destroy them along with my faith and hope to achieve them. But once I moved out and began to pursue my own life as I set out to find out who I was and what I could be, I started to take the necessary steps to make each of my dreams reality. Without dreams, our lives seem so lost and empty. It is dreams that give our lives that spark which then turns into a raging fire of desire to get out there and go after them.

Rebuilding our lives takes time. It is not something that happens right away. However, we need to remember that as the architects of our own lives, we now can create and design them into what we want them to be, making them even more beautiful than the past we left behind. Yes, there will be those who try to discourage us and bring us down but as long as we keep focused on what we hope to achieve, then nothing is impossible to reach. I know what it's like to be the underdog in life, to be the one that no one has any expectations for because they don't think we'll amount to much. As underdogs, we need to continue to rise above and prove to ourselves just what we can achieve in our own lives when we set our minds to it. The old bridges we must learn to burn so that we can build new bridges that will lead us to a better life and more promising future. So to all the people out there who have always been put down and told they won't get anywhere, stand strong and pursue your dreams. After all, the only person who can really kill your dream is you. Keep those dreams alive as you conceive them, envision them, nurture them, and allow them to grow till you see them in full bloom. As long as you have faith in yourself and believe in yourself, then nothing can stand in your way from turning your dreams into reality.

Jenna Kandyce Linch- July 28, 2009

Behind These Walls

So many questions weigh on her mind
As she approaches that point where herself she can't find.
Why does everyone think she's so strong
When she's not even sure where she does belong.

For years she's kept the pain locked inside
Her emotional side from the world she learned to hide.
What her heart really feels she doesn't know how to say
The motions she goes through are the same every day.

Subconsciously she tries to block out things that happened
Facing the truth, though, makes it impossible to pretend.
Still she fakes a smile everywhere she goes
Never letting on that inside her loneliness grows.

All around her, friends seem happy and content
But by traumatic events her life in half was bent.
Time passes by as she finds herself stuck in one place
Left behind, she's finishing last in life's race
She never really fit in with her peer group

Growing up too fast, her life was one chaotic loop.
For too long she's run away from all she knew
Continuing to search for something true.

Because of hurt, she only knows how to push people away
Her real emotions she fears she'll betray.
Distancing herself, her heart is guarded by walls she built
As she attempts to cover unwanted feelings of shame and guilt.

For years the secrets of her past have been kept safe from the outside
Living in silence, she didn't know in whom to confide.
Now as each day comes to an end, her walls threaten to fall apart
Exposing a fragile, bleeding, broken heart.

Can people handle the truth about her life
Or betraying her, will they leave in her back a knife?
There's only one way for her to find out
She must take that first step forward without a doubt.

In order to be free from the past, she can't let fear hold her back any longer
Breaking her silence will help make her stronger.
One shot is all she has to make things right
Too long she's struggled alone in this fight.

People who don't understand she can't worry about
When it comes to her life, they hold no clout.
Even if she must stand alone, she's ready to face her fear
There's nothing to lose with all she's overcome to get here.

This is her time to shine
No more walking on a thin line.
To make a difference she has a once in a lifetime chance
That means letting go of the past and moving on start to advance.

Most of her life these walls she's hid behind
Tearing them down, her way she's ready to find.
With her heart leading the way, she listens to her own voice
To be free and live her life is her choice.

The Life That You Have

I know it's not always easy to just let go and
move on
Especially when pain has left part of your heart
feeling gone.
People make assumptions based on your past
Judging you, they treat you like an outcast.

On a road filled with twists and turns you
walk alone
To the world you're just another stranger
unknown.
Behind your smile lies so much more
A story that people have not heard before.

Among the crowd, you desperately search for
your place
Yet you find yourself surrounded by many an
unfamiliar face.
With your past thrown at you, you wonder
where you belong
How do you make amends for those who have
done you wrong?

The question weighing on your mind is why
Instead of getting the truth, you're told a lie.
That you'll be like everyone else is what they
expect
Because the real truth they don't want anyone
to suspect.

Pretending nothing happened doesn't make it disappear
Facing it straight on, in the eye you must look your fear.
If you just stand still and do nothing you'll lose
Either dwell on the past or move forward is what you have to choose.

Closing your eyes, shut the rest of the world out for a while
Envisioning the future you want, your thoughts compile.
There's no limit to what you can achieve
When in your dreams you strongly believe.

No matter how rough our lives began, we always get a second chance
But we must seize the opportunity in order to advance.
One life is all that we get
So why waste it by looking back in regret?

How will we ever know what we can be
If past the horizons we don't see.
In each of us lays many strengths
To make a difference though we must be willing to travel great lengths

One road we traveled may have ended
However, following our hearts, we find ourselves on the path for which we were intended.
To live the life we've always wanted we can create

Because no matter where we've been, it's never too late.

Forget about what others think of you or say
Standing up for what you believe, the truth never be afraid to convey.
With your words and actions, on people's lives you can leave an impact
Inspiring them, you may encourage them to speak out and act.

All of us have a purpose in our lives to fulfill
But the moment will pass us by if we stand still.
This is our time to step up and make a difference
Breaking our silence, are we willing to go the distance?

Many stories have gone untold and many voices unheard
When we share our stories, we restore hope that's been shattered.
In this world we must continue standing strong
With the lives we have, let's right the wrong.

Never Alone

She sits alone, staring at the blank walls
Inside for someone to listen her heart calls.
Back down memory lane she's gone
In her mind, past memories play on.

Revisiting her past, she's taken to days of long ago
Things that she never wanted anyone to know.
For the path she once traveled was very dark
That part of her life became a dangerous part on which to embark.

As she looks back, she sees the wreckage of her life's chaos
Stolen innocence was her greatest loss.
All these years the haunting memories she's tried to suppress
Because she feared that of her people would think less.

Nothing happened were the words she learned to recite
Yet everyday home turned into a battlefield where she had to fight.
Often she found herself trapped on the warpath
Feeling the pain left from the aftermath.

With no one there to protect her, herself she had to defend

Threatened into silence, that everything was
fine she was forced to pretend.
This little girl grew up faster then one could
imagine
But with her remained the scars of sin.

A dark period of her life she entered
To some of the toughest times she encountered
to them she referred.
She found herself dangerously close to defeat
Into depression and self-infliction she did
retreat.

Brainwashing was her abusers' weapon of
choice
For they did not want her to use her voice.
Her self-esteem became greatly marred
Looking at her reflection, she saw an image
emotionally scarred.

Love in her life was non-existent
The girl nobody wanted, away she got sent.
She watched her life spiral out of control
As the effects of the damage done took its toll.

All alone many tears she cried
But those tears from everyone else she learned
to hide.
The burden of shame and guilt that was not
hers she bore
As into a million pieces her heart tore.

Her heart bleeds as she recalls the hate and violence
Just thinking about it makes her grow tense.
Exactly how she survived it she couldn't say how
Yet the pain from the past lingers on even now.

Much of her life she felt very isolated
Being a trapped victim she hated.
She was viewed as different because of her history
Beyond her past people chose not to see.

All of this she thinks about as she sits alone tonight
The miracle is that she lived because she decided to fight.
Yes, she could have quit and thrown her life away
Strong willed and stubborn, she chose in life to stay.

It took time for her to learn to love herself
Especially when for years her heart was on a shelf.
What she was made of she found
Discovering the strength within, she stood her ground.

What keeps her going is knowing her life holds so much more
Everyday as she pieces her heart together, hope and faith she's able to restore.

With the world her story she shares
Letting others out there know there's someone who cares.

So tonight, she walks out of that empty room, leaving her past behind
That she's not going to give up she made up her mind.
Like a phoenix, she rises above the ashes of her past
For she plans on rebuilding a life foundation that will last.

Even though she's been through a lot, she knows she's where she's supposed to be
Of her survival, her scars are her testimony.
Because of her experiences into a stronger woman she's grown
Now wherever she goes, she brings the message that no one is ever alone.

Because Of You

I was the type who in the shadows would hide
Due to an abusive past, stripped from me was all my pride.
On the outside looking in I remained
A history of violence left my heart stained.

I watched every dream be shattered
Just like a kite caught in a storm gets frayed and tattered.
Though I wore my heart on my sleeve, it crashed to the floor
With the pieces in disarray, I didn't recognize it anymore.

I often wondered if my life would ever be the same
Since for years I was a victim in a very cruel game.
My own demons I had to slay
Because no longer did this game I wish to play.

By myself I set out on a journey of healing
With so many past issues I found myself dealing.
In the dark I struggled to find my way
Unfortunately those in my life chose not to stay.

A few times along the path I tripped and fell
Only to pick myself up again, knowing I had a story to tell.

I wondered how many other survivors were
out there
Waiting for the chance to also be able to share.

That I had a mission to fulfill I knew
For just as I once waited, many souls awaited
rescue.
Yet on this journey I felt alone
Parts of my life still lay in pieces after being hit
by an emotional cyclone.

I thought nobody would understand all I had
suffered
Especially when the haunting memories often
recurred.
Thoughts of what you put me through came
back to mind
The truth is that while you abandoned me, I
was the one who really left you behind.

You may have caused me so much pain
But in the end I was the one who had more to
gain.
What didn't kill me definitely made me
stronger
Thanks to you, in life I became one hell of a
fighter.

Over my life you wanted absolute control
Standing up to you, I decided the wrong part
for me to play was the victim role.
The day I broke completely free took you by
surprise

Your plan for me I figured I'd change and revise.

The unbreakable you cannot possibly break
No longer afraid of you, the truth I refused to fake.
After my wings began to heal, I took flight
Taking a step forward, my story I started to write.

You thought I'd never make it out alive
Well, your mistake was underestimating my will to survive.
My voice I found again
It wasn't a matter of if I'd escape, it was all a matter of when.

Something beautiful from the ashes rose
Saving lives and reaching out, I decided to fight alongside other heroes.
A whole new meaning this life of mine holds
Now I watch as the map to my purpose unfolds.

I'm not that scared little girl of yesterday
With the help of other survivors and friends, I've found my way.
My calling in life I'll continue to serve
Because if it's one thing I have, it's nerve.

By limitations I am not confined

For carrying out and achieving greater things
in life I was designed.
I've discovered the real strength in me after all
I went through
And it's all because of you.

Tears In The Dark

She sits all alone in the dark, tears streaming down her face
Wishing there was someone who could give her a much needed embrace.
Here she is after another terrifying night
In which she was a victim in a ruthless fight.

For the time, she's safe from him locked behind this door
From a lost battle, her body still feels soar.
She always said she would not marry someone like her dad
Yet somehow she ended up with a man who treats her just as bad.

As she rocks back and forth, she remembers those days as a young girl
The events of those times in her mind begin to unfurl.
Most nights she couldn't get any sleep
Because after her parents fought, she'd hear her mom weep.

In her room or bathroom, her mom would hide
Never coming out or letting anyone inside.
Of her former self she became a shadow
While into a deep sea of depression she sunk low.

The things she watched her mom go through were unspeakable

Of such cruelty she never knew one could be capable.
So many times she wished she could comfort her mom and wipe her tears
Living in a house turned war zone, she too had her own fears.

She never knew how her mom felt until she found herself in the same situation
When her own marriage became a battlefield on which she couldn't win.
At first everything seemed to go all right
But things changed as her husband grew into a stranger who filled her with fright.

Although he said he loved her, she knew it wasn't okay
For love shouldn't hurt and feel this way.
Every time she took him back and stayed, the abuse grew worse
This marriage was not a blessing but rather a curse.

With his brainwashing, her self-esteem he destroyed
Soon left in her heart was an empty void.
He threatened her and manipulated her into silence
So she'd lock herself up in the bathroom to escape his violence.

As she looked in the mirror, she saw a bit of her mom staring back

Suddenly she realized how her mom felt after each attack.
All to well she knew of the tears that were cried
The feelings of guilt and shame making one feel they'd emotionally died.

Until now, she never understood why her mom stayed
It was the insecurity of being alone that made her afraid.
She allowed him to have complete control
So her and her daughter were trapped in the victim role.

Wiping her tears, she doesn't want to make that same mistake
Leaving and getting out is the chance she's willing to take.
The pain, the endless tears, the lack of love are not worth it anymore
She deserves better then to relive her life from before.

Her mom she chooses not to take after
What she wants is a life filled with love, hope, and laughter.
For to her it is better on a journey alone to embark
Then to keep crying these tears in the dark.

Our Time Is Now

We live in a world where lives from abuse are torn apart
Behind fake smiles lies many a broken heart.
Their eyes though tell a different story
One that they are afraid for others to see.

People don't know about the tears they've cried
Or when threatened into silence, for their abusers they lied.
No one was around to witness the violent fights
Fearing for their lives, they spent many sleepless nights.

Their innocence was stolen at a young age
They were victims caught in the midst of someone else's rage.
But their voices went unheard
Because using brainwashing, the abuser ensured they didn't say a word.

Covering scars and bruises, they hid them out of sight
For they wanted people to believe everything was all right.
The stories they told they rehearsed beforehand
Knowing the real truth others wouldn't understand.

So what took place in their homes no one suspected
Nor could they imagine the pain suffered because these lives were unprotected.
To the victims, it felt as if they were sentenced to a life of hell
Forever suffering alone emotionally since there was no one to tell.

Yet some of us remember those days all too well
Even though we escaped from our cell.
Fresh still, those memories remain in our mind
For the abuse left its own scars behind.

As survivors, we once found ourselves on the other side
The ones that learned to recognize when to run and hide.
Danger seemed to surround us everywhere we went
Our lives in total isolation were spent.

Many times we felt alone and afraid
While we watched our light dim and fade.
We yearned to tell someone what was going on
But if we did, we weren't sure if we'd live to see the dawn.

Somehow we managed to finally break away and leave
The lies we exposed even when others they tried to deceive.
Obstacles in our lives we overcame

Giving back to those who hurt us the blame.

Now that we have emerged stronger, we can help those still lost
Before it gets worse and death becomes the cost.
We were once in their place so we are able to relate
Their lives we can save, preventing them from ending in a tragic fate.

These silent voices deserve a chance to be heard
For we believe them and know their stories aren't absurd.
The truth about abuse we need to expose
Our abusers no longer have say since a new life without them we chose.

But those still trapped are looking for somewhere to turn
As heroes and role models, they look to us as from our stories they learn.
Why wait any longer when there are many lives to save
Speaking out, our time is now as a path to freedom we pave.

Saving Grace

You see them everyday
The strangers who look at you and smile when you pass their way.
But you never suspect anything since you can't see behind the mask
Not knowing something's wrong, it doesn't cross your mind to ask.

Their hearts they may not wear on their sleeve
Deep inside, it's understanding for their story they wish to receive.
Silent they've remained for so long
Even though on the outside they appear to be strong.

The truth about their past they aren't sure how to convey
Because they fear people will leave without hearing what they have to say.
The last thing they want is to be treated like an outcast
Experience has taught them that people are quick to judge a person's past.

Emotions they've learned to hide
For they were told to be tough and suck it up when they cried.
Far away they push others since they're use to fighting on their own
To them it feels better sometimes to be alone.

Yet there's another side to them waiting to be shown
A part that to everyone else has gone unknown.
Behind those walls they set up lies a fragile soul
One on which years of silence has taken its toll.

Sure they seem so confident
That's because they don't want to be viewed as any different.
For someone willing to listen they seek
A person who will keep their story confidential and not let it leak.

Knowing who to trust is the toughest issue they face
After being hurt and abused, their inner child they're learning to embrace.
It's hard to let people close when they were betrayed
They think that everyone will leave since no one ever stayed.

All they hear is how they're strong and will make it through this time
How rich they'd be if every time that was said to them they had a dime.
Of course they know they're strong or they wouldn't be here today
What they need to hear are the words, "It's going to be okay."

The more their emotions are held inside, the more they fall apart
Until into a million pieces shatters their heart.
When they face darkness and no one's there, they lose hope
Often finding themselves at the end of their rope.

Feeling lost, they aren't sure where to turn
Since between real friends and fake friends, it can be hard to discern.
Some give up, thinking there's no escape from the pain
Staying silent and locking emotions inside creates quite a strain.

The truth is that everyone needs someone to be there
All by themselves a heavy burden they shouldn't have to bear.
That someone cares is what they need to know
So they don't continue to live their life in a dark shadow.

Even those who seem strong go through a rough time
They too have their own mountains to climb.
Of pain and suffering they've had their share
But other people's broken hearts they're expected to repair.

Our leaders and role models we shouldn't take for granted
They also have hearts that could be mended.
After all, they are human like all the rest
In their own lives they constantly get put to the test.

Nobody can do everything on their own
To battle the storms, they shouldn't be left alone.
Behind those smiles, for help their hearts cry out
Desperately longing for someone to hear what their feelings are about.

Many people walk on life's narrow ledge
They get closer and closer to slipping off the edge.
To them we need to reach out a hand
Letting them know that we do understand.

It only takes a listening ear
As well as showing them we are sincere.
No more lives should be lost because people don't see anyone there
Taking them under our wing, the tears with them we should share.

So many hurting souls out there wait
Praying that it's not too late.
Standing with them on the battlefield, let's fight by their side
Hope and faith for them we can provide.

Leave no one behind
Taking their hand, their way we'll help them find.
Maybe the past we can't erase, but together the future we can embrace
For those feeling lost and trapped may we be their saving grace.

Little Girl Lost

I saw her again today
A little girl sitting alone who seemed to have lost her way.
Staring straight ahead, not one word did she speak
But there were traces of tears visible on her cheek.

She couldn't have been more then ten years old
Trying to stay warm, she shivered against the cold.
A teddy bear she hugged tight
I wondered who let this precious child out of their sight.

Surely someone must be missing this child
By now a missing persons report should have been filed.
As I watched, no one seemed to notice she was there
They kept walking as if they didn't even care.

This was no place for a little girl to be out here alone on the street
Approaching her, I spotted the bruises where it looked like she'd been beat.
It was then that I realized she didn't want to be found
Wherever she came from, someone had used her as a punching bag on which to pound.

Looking at the innocent soul, memories of my own childhood came back
How I often witnessed the abusive way in which my dad would attack.
Too afraid to move, in the corner of my room I'd sit
Through the walls I could hear each hit.

Hugging my teddy bear close, silent tears I would cry
Praying my mom would be safe and not die.
So many horrifying things I saw
From the pain my heart was left bleeding and raw.

In this little girl, I glimpsed a part of myself
Someone had thrown her away, putting her heart on the shelf.
Betraying her trust, a person close to her made her suffer pain
It angered me that from hurting a child pleasure a person did gain.

This child should have been cherished and surrounded by love
For like all children, she was an angel sent from above.
Yet her they failed to defend and protect
The bruises served as evidence to the abuse's after effect.

Tears welled in my eyes as I could only imagine the pain she'd been through

Just a scared little girl who didn't know where to go or what to do.
So far from home she'd run away
What had happened to no one would she say.

She deserved to grow up in a home safe from harm
For any loving, caring person would fall in love with her charm.
A chance to enjoy being a kid she should be given
Her childhood hiding in fear she shouldn't be livin.

For this little girl I could feel my heart ache
Her innocence someone ruthlessly and mercilessly decided to take.
Next to her I took a seat
Determined that her past she would not repeat.

The tears I wiped from her face
Without saying a word, I wrapped her in a warm embrace.
I vowed to protect this little girl lost
Keeping her safe from harm no matter what the cost.

A Survivor's Resolution

As I look back over my painful past, I know it's one I didn't choose
It was never my fault that a part of my childhood I had to lose.
What matters is that I'm working hard to get my life back
Finally gaining control again and getting back on track.

Over the years, many lessons I've learned
But deep inside me to find myself is what I yearned.
Breaking the chains holding me prisoner proved to be tough
In my heart though, to start over, I knew that wouldn't be enough.

My life I had to completely rebuild
To the temptations to give up and quit I could not yield.
Approaching the crossroads of my life, a road I had to pick
Igniting a new fire, I put out the flame of the past and cut the wick.

My heart I decided to follow
Taking the things I learned, I allowed myself to grow.
A bright, shiny future I envisioned in my mind
Getting out there, my dreams I ventured to find.

I knew the odds were stacked against me
However, knowing no limits, I was determined to be free.
Once I found myself drifting far from shore
Holding on to everything I had, I made my way back believing in something more.

Those who hurt me I chose to forgive
Because harboring hate in my heart wouldn't let me freely live.
Myself I began to truly love
When I doubted myself, to keep moving forward I gave myself a shove.

Stay stuck in the past or keep moving forward
I didn't have to contemplate
Because to live the life I always wanted to I knew it wasn't too late.
There were times I thought I couldn't go on
I kept moving forward though when everyone else was gone.

What mattered was not where I had once been in life
All that counted was that I rose above the strife.
Even when I fell down, I got back on my feet
Determined not to ever surrender to the negative and let it have me beat.

To make it through the hard times, my outlook I changed
Staying focused on my goals and dreams, a new life for myself I arranged.

Taking risks and chances, I knew I had nothing to lose
Failure wasn't an option I was about to choose.

A promise I made to myself as my life I turned around
To my past I would no longer be bound.
Those chapters I closed forever
Writing a new and improved sequel became my endeavor.

The old days I left behind
As the real me I began to find.
Making the most of my life my heart I continued to follow
Gaining freedom and obtaining happiness meant having to let go.

Now today I give with all I have to give
Enjoying every moment of this life I live.
Not worrying about those who hurt me, I love with all I have to love
For like a phoenix, from the ashes of the past I rise above.

Beauty From The Ashes

The world may not understand what we've been through
Often we go unrecognized for the work that we do.
Our past sometimes makes things complicated
Going unnoticed we feel we're not appreciated.

People only see what's on the surface
Anything different they consider a menace.
Seeing only what they want to see, they never look beyond
Gathered in their own little groups, with outsiders they cut the bond.

To the subject of abuse society turns a blind eye
Attempting to cover the truth with lie after lie.
About the damaging effects the rest go uneducated
As survivors on the low end of the scale we're rated.

In their minds, our battle scars stick way out
The stories of what we suffered they question and doubt.
Ignorance leads them to act superior
Being constantly judged, we begin feeling inferior.

All our insecurities our reflections tend to reveal

Returning are the fears that we've managed to conceal.
Thinking back on those painful days we ask why
For back then our wings were damaged where we could not fly.

We wonder what's left that's real
The only thing we can do is allow our wounds to heal.
Yet from everything we feel so far away
But we continue to take life day by day.

The mountains we face are pretty steep
Using our strength, we climb them, knowing what lies on the other side is worth its keep.
Engraved on our hearts is the map to our destiny
Possibilities past the horizons we see.

For too long we've hidden in the shadows
At times in our lives we reached various lows.
Memories caught up with us when them we tried to outrun
Dark days blocked out the sun.

Despite hardships, through the storms we persevered
Facing our fears straight on when they closed in and neared.
Inside each of us a fire burned bright
We answered the call to go and fight.

The hearts of warriors beat strong and true

Uniting together, we found we numbered more then just a few.
With courage surging through our veins, we charged on the battlefield
Protecting the innocent from harm, around them we formed a shield.

Our mission became to right the wrong
Discovering we were exactly where we belong.
From our past for this battle we were prepared
Not letting anything stop us, going above and beyond we dared.

In this fight we are warriors at heart
Our call to duty is protecting innocent lives from being shattered apart.
The message we bring with us is one of hope
To those barely holding on we throw a rope.

A lesson of self-love and forgiveness we teach
Our hand out to those who are lost we reach.
Their battered wings we help repair
Showing them there are others who care.

The worst times in our lives are over now
Never returning to them is what we vow.
It doesn't matter how others see us but how ourselves we view
We grew stronger because of what we went through.

Our scars bear testimony to that strength
Just to make it this far we traveled a great length.

At one point, negativity was all we saw around
Turning it into something positive, we proved
beauty from the ashes can be found.

Heroes Around The World

From different backgrounds they emerge
Of changing history they're on the verge.
Their stories may not be the same
But for themselves they're trying to make a name.

Where they started out in life no one really knows
Yet it is courage and determination in them that shows.
The sacrifices they make they ask for nothing in return
From their lives, though, so much we can learn.

They've seen and been through things that others can't begin to imagine
When it came to breaking free, they were told victory they wouldn't win.
Those words fell upon deaf ears
Giving it their all, they set out to conquer their fears.

Unscathed, they walked through the fire
Finding strength within to push on even when they started to tire.
The odds stacked against them served as their motivation
To others they would become an inspiration.

Forward was the only direction they knew
Their destiny they chose to bravely pursue.

They picked themselves back up when they fell
Of their triumph later generations would tell.

They were marked as the outcasts of society
Passion for living is what they continued to see.
For their future they fought
Not allowing negativity to leave them distraught.

Facing the enemy, they knew what they were up against
Behind insecurity and doubt they could not be fenced.
Being different may have set them apart
Respect they received though for following their heart.

The path they traveled led them to greater places
Today it is their legacy that their following generation embraces.
So who are these people who have left their footprints on history
They are the survivors who paved the way by breaking free.

Survivors turned heroes is what they are
In their lives they are still going far.
Reaching out to others, a difference they make
Rewriting their history, they don't repeat any past mistake.

By their character and traits they are measured

The message of hope they bring by many is treasured.
As role models and leaders they're revered
Believing in them, for them people have cheered.

Everyday so many lives they save
In the eyes of those saved they're courageous and brave.
A new meaning to life they've brought
They incorporate the lessons of love and healing they were taught.

Their stories they pass on
Forever their legends will continue even after they're gone.
To make the world a better place, these heroes around the world unite
Protecting the innocent from harm, together they fight.

Without You

The shattered picture frame reminds me of
how my life lay in disarray
What I thought would be happily after didn't
turn out that way.
For a while I walked around feeling numb
inside
Everyone looked at me as if I had all ready
died.

I thought I had this wonderful future planned
out
The day my marriage ended, I suddenly was
overcome by self-doubt.
My broken heart I put under lock and key
Insecurity made me question what was wrong
with me.

Your voice in my mind I could hear
At one time because of you I lived in fear.
A part of my life you stole
Finding myself a victim, I started losing
control.

For a time I stayed to try to make things right
But you had given up and let me go without a
fight.
The love you claimed to have for me you lost
Being thrown away was the cost.

I found myself facing a destination unknown
Wondering how I'd make it through this on my
own.

My world became this dark, lonely place
It could only be described as a time I felt I had fallen from grace.

Here I was living my life on the rebound
Nowhere though could self-love and acceptance be found.
Nearing a dead end I knew if I continued, I'd crash and burn
Yet to turn around would mean going back to somewhere I wished to never return.

One way or another my life I had to begin to rebuild
For it was the only way that these wounds would ever be healed.
I didn't want to be stuck in a tragic past
Because over my life a gloomy shadow it cast.

A goodbye to the past I said
Focusing my sight on the road ahead.
I must now turn this page
Otherwise, I'll only be trapped in an emotional cage.

I won't look back on yesterday
In my heart, I have faith that everything will be okay.
Letting go is the only way to move on
Though it may hurt a bit, my hope is not gone.

It took me leaving to discover the strength in me

Learning to love and accept myself, that it wasn't my fault I had to see.
What happened cannot be denied
The truth I will no longer hide.

My life I have taken back
Having a new perspective, I'm on the right track.
Nothing do I regret
The lessons I learned I will never forget.

Taking chances is what my life is about
With confidence, I have replaced my fear and doubt.
I grew stronger because of what you put me through
Standing on my own, I know I can make it without you.

Now That I Know

As I look back on my life, I've seen how so many changes took place
Most of them on my own I had to face.
Life for me was not an easy walk in the park
I suffered in silence through times that were very dark.

I grew up faster than most kids do
Enduring abuse that no child should have to go through.
Back then, there was no one around for me to tell
So I remained trapped in a nightmarish hell.

Everything just fell completely apart
My parents would fight and then the abuse would start.
Going to my mom's rescue, I'd protect her so she wouldn't get hurt
Unfortunately for me there wasn't any alert.

As a kid, I ran away for a few hours so I couldn't be found
Escaping to a secret spot, I made sure nobody was around.
Left alone with my thoughts, my feelings I'd write
Looking out over the water, I wondered what lay hidden out of sight.

Most nights into my pillow tears I cried

Wishing I could run away forever and hide.
That they didn't want me they made clear
I heard the cutting remarks they said when I was near.

Along with my writings, my self-esteem they destroyed
Even after I left home, in my heart I felt a void.
For a long time myself I set out to find
Yet I seemed to be falling way behind.

Due to feelings of shame and guilt, the real me I didn't know how to accept
The secrets buried deep within me I still kept.
Letting anyone close is what really made me afraid
Too many times by people I trusted I was betrayed.

Although it wasn't my fault, I carried the blame
Into my life struggles with insecurity came.
From drinking to self-infliction, I tried to get rid of the pain
Nothing worked for it left me broken without anything to gain.

Memories lingered that I could not erase
I lost my dignity and grace.
Then one day I realized I didn't want to feel like this anymore
Thus I began searching for an open door.

My broken heart didn't heal over night

I knew that to regain control of my life I'd have to fight.
From the wreckage, the pieces of my heart I retrieved
As I began fitting them together, self-love and acceptance I received.

My eyes were opened to the truth about my past
Acknowledging it was never my fault became the first step to a future that would last.
For the first time everything in me I could see
Revealed beneath the scars was so much strength and beauty.

I am still healing even today
But I have finally found my way.
The things I went through I'll never forget
Now when I look back, it isn't with regret.

In so many ways I have grown
Learning that in this fight I'm not alone.
I'm no longer afraid to take a chance
As I take life up on its opportunities, my own life I enhance.

Speaking out is my choice
They can't silence my voice.
A fighter and survivor, I'm here to stay
Now that I know I'm not alone, the truth I'll continue to say

From One Survivor To Another

So many memories play in your mind
As you think back to the life you left behind.
All you knew then was so much sorrow
Sometimes wondering if you'd survive to see tomorrow.

You never told anyone about what you were going through
For if your abuser found out, you feared what they'd do.
It was better to keep silent than risk the consequence
Daily you suffered through pain that grew intense.

No one ever saw the tears you cried
Growing up in a broken home, your emotional side you learned to hide.
Why this was happening to you, you didn't understand
Hurting, people who wanted to help and get close you banned.

A part of your life from you they stole
Brainwashing and threats were their methods of control.
When it came to what you wanted to do, you had no say
Finding strength within, you finally escaped for good one day.

Yet being on your own hasn't proved to be easy
Some days the light at the end of the tunnel can be hard to see.
Nightmares and flashbacks take place when you least expect
Reminding you how much the damage still does affect.

Secrets burn inside you that you thought you buried
The truth is that throughout your life, them you've carried.
Your story has never fully been told
Because you were afraid if people knew, they'd act cold.

At times, you just want to run away from it all
Feeling weary, you're tired of always taking the fall.
There are moments you question if your life is real
The one thing you desire is from the pain to heal.

You're not exactly sure where to start
After all, you had your heart torn apart.
Can you get your life back after all that's happened
Or is it too late and this is the end?

My fellow survivors, there's something I wish to say

The healing process you must take day by day.
I know what it's like to have past demons taunt
Insecurities from those days sometimes haunt.

I've been in darkness before
Falling into depression, I couldn't find the open door.
I wondered what my life held
Because in my mind, I heard the voices of my abusers saying I'd failed.

I felt like giving up and giving in
Thinking there was no way I would ever win.
But I remembered the strength inside me
Knowing I had the courage to break free.

I was afraid to speak out too
Not wanting people to think less of me if my story they knew.
Taking a chance, I knew I had nothing to lose
Freedom for myself I decided to choose.

As a survivor, your story can help so many more
You can relate to them since you've been there before.
By sharing your testimony, respect you'll earn
Encouraging others so in speaking out they may take their turn.

No longer are you trapped in the victim role
You used your strength to get out and take back control.
You're living proof that one can survive

Because after all you have endured, you're still here and alive.

The answer never lies in quitting and giving in
It's not too late because you have an opportunity to rebuild your life again.
Your future doesn't need to reflect your past
This is your time to write a new beginning that will last.

Sure, what you suffered you won't ever forget
Don't live your life though by looking back in regret.
In all you do, continue to stand strong
When you follow your heart, you can never go wrong.

Always remember you're beautiful the way you are
You should take pride in knowing you've made it this far.
It's okay to let go because you don't need to carry feelings of shame
What happened was not your fault so you are not the one to blame.

Never give up in this fight
The world needs warriors to stand up for what's right.
As a survivor, to others you are an inspiration
Sharing your story, to keep holding on you give them motivation.

DREAM Acronym

Dare

Reach

Embrace

Achieve

Motivate

When No One's Around

On the outside she remains strong
Seeing her smile, no one suspects anything is wrong.
Even when things are rough, she tries to stay positive
Though at times, it can be a struggle to keep having the will to live.

Her true emotions she manages to hide
Afraid to open up, exposing a fragile, vulnerable side.
She travels through life everyday the same
Blending in with the crowd, she doesn't allow anyone to know her name.

Surrounded by so many people she still feels lost and alone
For the actions of those who have hurt her, she's had to atone.
Although those days are gone, the memories linger on in her mind
Replaying over and over again, they continue to rewind.

From her past she's trying to run away
But she can't escape a part of her that is there to stay.
Edged into her skin, scars from her heart show
Yet about that side of her she won't let anyone know.

When it comes to letting people near, she's all out of trust
What was done to her in her past was not fair or just.
Many times the intense emotional pain has made her want to die
Unanswered always remains the question why.

Blocking everything out, on those dark times she tries not to reflect
As hard as she pretends it doesn't bother her, she feels the after effect.
To run and hide becomes her first instinct
Because to a haunting past she's tired of being linked.

She knows she can't continue to keep emotions locked inside
Her life is turning into an emotional roller coaster ride.
The problem is that of this ride she's losing control
Up ahead lies an empty, black hole.

Away from destruction she attempts to steer
Wondering if onto a different track she can veer.
The dangers and perils flashing before her are all too real
Old wounds tear open that have not yet started to heal.

Her life is the only thing she wants back

Yet she's not sure if she has the strength to withstand this attack.
Temptation to quit and surrender calls her name
Bringing with it reminders of guilt and shame.

She searches for a way out
Refusing to be conquered by this self-doubt.
By the insecurities of a time long ago she won't be overtaken
Standing strong and remembering who she is, she can't be shaken.

She thinks about how far she's made it in life
How she's fought all these years to rise above the strife.
If she could beat the odds against her, then fear she will defeat
No matter what happens, the painful past of long ago she doesn't have to repeat.

Releasing her emotions, she hugs her teddy bear
With him her tears she chooses to share.
Another battle she's won as more strength inside her she found
These are just some of the past demons she fights when no one's around.

Wishing You Were Here

(In Loving Memory of My Honorary Dad, Alan McEwen Who Passed Away September 1, 2008)

I found out the news tonight
In shock, I couldn't believe that what I was hearing could be right.
With the tragic news I am trying to deal
That you're gone though just doesn't seem real.

I keep asking myself why
Wishing I could have had the chance to say goodbye.
My heart aches with grief knowing you are no longer here
Yet since you live in my heart, you will always be near.

Even if it was for a short time, I'm glad I knew you
The rough times in my life you pulled me through.
You came into my life for a reason
Reaching out a hand to me when I had fallen.

The dad I never had you became
Guiding me through the storms, my life you helped me reclaim.
Knowing my story didn't make you think any less of me

The strength inside me you helped me see.

Always believing in me, my dreams you encouraged me to chase
You walked beside me when my steps I had to retrace.
Because of you I learned the meaning of life
Never once did you leave when I faced so much strife.

So many valuable precious lessons you taught
Back into my life hope you brought.
Taking my hand, you pulled be back to my feet
On life's battlefield you fought beside me even when I wanted to retreat.

In life, you always looked on the bright side
You were the honorary dad in whom I could confide.
I still remember your wise words of advice
And the conversations we had together were so nice.

No matter what I was going through, you made time to be there
With your positive attitude you lifted me out of my despair.
The struggles I had you seemed to understand
Accepting me for who I was, perfection you didn't demand.

The light you shined in my life with others I will share
Using the lessons you taught, broken hearts I'll help repair.
I am a better, stronger woman because you never gave up on me
You showed me that even in hard times there does exist beauty.

You touched the lives of so many around
Blessed to know you, a true friend in you we found.
You left footprints on our hearts that we won't forget
A great example for all of us you set.

Though it hurts to say goodbye, you're not really gone
For your memory in our hearts will forever live on.
A piece of yourself you left behind
In our hearts, it's your love we can still find.

I hope you know how much I love you and miss you
Making you proud, my goals and dreams I'll continue to pursue.
Right now I'm wishing you were here
But I know I don't have to look that far to know you're always near.

Extraordinary

You look in the mirror, not sure you recognize the person you see
There's always someone else people want you to be.
Your real story you don't wish them to know
So only certain parts of yourself you allow to show.

Smiling, you act as if nothing is wrong
With the in crowd you yearn to belong.
Everything in your past you've learned to hide well
Any information regarding those days you never volunteer to tell.

Some secrets are better left untold
Because if they got out, people would act cold.
A regular life you desire to lead
But you fear it won't happen if your true story others read.

For a long time you've fought alone on life's battlefield
Every dream you had was killed.
With no place to call home, you drifted from day to day
Always searching to find your way.

Somewhere out there you lost yourself
Your heart long ago was placed on a shelf.

The memories of where you came from you could never outrun
Weary from each mile traveled, you wonder if your life is done.

The strength that lies within your soul you underestimate
You had the courage to leave a dangerous situation before it was too late.
Deep inside, that things could get better you continued to believe
Taking back your life, your dreams and goals you set out to achieve.

You took the pieces of your life, deciding to rebuild
Moving on, you chose to let your broken heart be healed.
The past once holding you back you left behind
A new start in life you knew you had to find.

As a survivor, you've felt so much pain
But power over you was something you refused to let them gain.
With everything you had left you fought back
Those who hurt you never expected you to attack.

Even when faced with challenges, those chains you broke
Under pressure you never once did choke.
You did what you had to in order to survive
Fighting hard to stay alive

It doesn't matter what others want you to be
What matters is the way in which yourself you see.
To get this far trials and obstacles you overcame
The things you endured were not your fault so you shouldn't feel shame.

You've made the most of your life
Beating the odds, you rose above the strife.
Your story you don't have to hide
There are many others out there who are on your side.

Take a look at where you once were to where you are today
From victim to survivor you've certainly come a long way.
In the mirror a beautiful person you should see
After all you went through, to still be standing strong makes you extraordinary.

Along This Road

In many ways I've watched my life change
Facing the world on my own, for myself a new beginning I had to arrange.
I was put through one long childhood trial
While those who hurt me lived in denial.

For them they wanted me to lie
Not caring that I was left to emotionally die.
Silence became the only thing I knew
At that time, I didn't know what to do.

Only a child, I watched my world shatter apart
Suffering through the pain, broken into pieces laid my heart.
Instead of being loved and cherished, they threw me to the side
Everything I felt inside I learned to hide.

I wanted to run away and never return
For in that house violence and cruelty were lessons I had to learn.
No one ever came to my rescue
Because what was going on nobody else knew.

The untold secrets never got out
People didn't know what the family was really about.
Against them, myself I had to defend and protect

As I tried to deal with each damaging after effect.

I traveled through darkness
Not able to find myself in the emotional mess.
Even after I escaped, I felt lost and alone
Still holding back and hesitating to let the truth be known.

When I ventured to share my emotions, I was told to just be strong
As if people didn't care what was really wrong.
Speaking out proved to be quite an effort
Since those who didn't understand were quite judgmental and curt.

Conquering my fears was the only way I could move on
Even though the memories weren't gone.
I knew I couldn't live in silence and misery anymore
Breaking the chains of the past, I finally found the open door.

From the wounds left behind, I'm allowing myself to heal
Sharing my story, I want the world to know that abuse is very real.
With every step I take more strength I gain
Though I may face hard times, the sun always shines after the rain.

The scars I bear I no longer view as ugly

Of my survival in life they give a testimony.
What I went through doesn't make me worthless or different
For a reason into this world I was sent.

I've made it this far and I'm not about to give in
I fought hard to take back my life so victory I could win.
Where I started out in life I won't ever forget
But I don't want to waste my life living it with regret.

Going forward, I have no need to look behind
I use my past experiences to reach out, hoping that their voices others can find.
As I continue to believe in myself, out of the darkness I've found my way
Along this road I'm traveling, while I still heal, I look to a brighter day.

Secret Untold

Far from home she finds herself tonight
Having managed to barely escape another violent fight.
Now she's in an unfamiliar place
Ready for a new life to face.

She knows she can't go back home
It's better to be on the roam.
Back there her heart cannot be found
For it turned into a war zone where she fought to stand her ground.

The words he said to her she can still hear
Even though she left, it's as if his presence is near.
By the man she loved she was betrayed
He became a stranger of whom she grew afraid.

Daily with makeup the black eyes she had to conceal
The truth about the bruises to no one would she reveal.
With terror her life he reigned
Pleasure from the pain he put her through he gained.

Every aspect of her life he controlled

Threatening to hurt her even more if anyone she told.
She felt trapped as if in a prison cell
Fearing what he would do, she never did tell.

Her friends all thought they were in love
They told her she was lucky to be with an angel from above.
Little did they know about the tears he made her cry
Or how he broke her down till she started to emotionally die.

He had everyone fooled on the outside
With his well-known reputation, his other side he could hide.
Once he got home, a different person he became
When things went wrong, it was her he would blame.

Walking on eggshells, she never knew when he'd attack
Around him, she constantly had to watch her back.
Too many times she gave him a chance when his lies she believed
Yet each time worse beatings she received.

By staying, her life she would lose
For her freedom, leaving was the risk she decided to choose.
Her life she didn't want to live begging for

In her heart she knew she deserved something more.

Without a word, out of the house she crept
This promise of forever was better left unkept.
Never looking back she left everything behind
The only prayer she breathed was that her he would never find.

Into the night she continued to drive
Thankful she was able to make it out alive.
To that way of life she will never return
Her safety is her main concern.

Now is her time to get a new start
With faith and hope she'll rebuild the pieces of her life that were torn apart.
Taking back control of her life, onto a better future she grabs hold
Finally ready to speak out and release her secret that's gone untold.

Cruising Down Life's Highway

In life I've traveled through many a different state
During the early stages, I witnessed much violence and hate.
Just starting out on this journey and all ready facing bumps that were rough
I felt as if I had seen and heard more than enough.

Venturing out on my own, a new road I took
As I changed scenery, I developed a different outlook.
Instead of darkness, I began to see light up ahead
Choosing to follow the signs, I wondered where this alternate route led.

Off into the horizon I found myself stare
Looking back on where I came from I didn't dare.
At a crossroads, the path started to divide
I picked the one less traveled as I sat back to enjoy the ride.

The steering wheel was placed in my hand
That I would be in control of getting to my new destination I began to understand.
Cautiously I approached every bend
Careful not to crash into a dangerous dead end.

Through stormy weather I drove
Battling the fierce winds, my way through the twists and turns I wove.
Obstacles tried to block my view
But that the sun always shines again I knew.

Continuing to drive on, I saw things I hadn't seen before
I gained a new perspective as I realized my life held so much more.
Once stuck in traffic, I nearly missed opportunities
Since following others led me to toll booths where I paid high fees.

Now out here I was surrounded by fresh air where I could breathe
All the pollution got left behind when the main roads I decided to leave.
With the sun shining bright, the view suddenly became so clear
Staying on the road I was on, off it I did not veer.

Shortcuts others took saved time but led to nowhere great
Taking my time traveling the scenic route, I knew where I was going I wouldn't be late.
Everyone else may have wanted quick and easy
However, finding the path right for me, my journey grew light and breezy.

I saw my peers pull over as they broke down on the side
Yet here I cruised on an open road, knowing I had nothing to hide.
Relaxing, I observed all the beautiful sights
In the distance I could still see those guiding lights.

The places may have changed, but never once did I switch over to another lane
Following my heart, I remembered if I didn't venture out nothing would I gain.
When others joined in caravans, I stuck it out
Because that I needed to find my own destination I had no doubt.

I'm still staying true to the road in life I'm on
Even when things fall apart and those I once knew are gone.
I've left the old days far behind
Finally the point in my journey where I should be I've started to find.

As I follow the map of my life, I know right where I belong
Listening to my heart and following its directions, I can't go wrong.
Through the tunnels and into the light I've emerged to see a better day
My future looks bright as I cruise down life's highway.

Turn Around

Turn around and take a look at me
Do you recognize the person you now see?
I've changed in more ways than you know
No longer am I the leading role in your cruel show.

For years my every move you controlled
Under your tyranny my life began to fold.
To you I was only a puppet on strings that you pulled
With an iron fist you mercilessly ruled.

In my heart and soul fear you instilled
As my days with danger and peril you filled.
Robbing me of emotions, you mocked and scorned me in every way
For your cruel actions I had to pay.

Tormenting me with threats, you were relentless
Foolishly I stayed even when my life became one big mess.
To make you happy I followed your harsh script
Into a million pieces my heart ripped.

Under heavy chains my heart was locked
To a dead end led the road that I walked.
From existence I felt myself begin to fade
Smiling on the outside, a different person I portrayed.

Covering for you, lies I would recite
Sometimes I wondered if I'd live to see daylight.
A pawn I became in your game
One in which I had so much shame.

Gaining my freedom is what I yearned
About my escape plan you never learned.
The day arrived where I was gone for good
Leaving behind my nightmarish childhood.

Years later here I stand
This time it's you who from my life is being banned.
I grew stronger because of you
I'm not the scared, silent kid you once knew.

Now that I've found my voice, I won't be silenced
Breaking free, to a life of pain and misery I refused to be sentenced.
The fight to survive still continues
Living for me though is what I choose.

You couldn't destroy my spirit
Because to my dreams and goals there's no limit.
I love this life I now live
Fighting to get my freedom, the past served as my motive.

Thanks to you I know what not to do
I will never put others through what you put me through.

The strings that tied me to you I burned
After your lifestyle, my own life won't be patterned.

Turn around and look at my face
This is not the face of one who's fallen from grace.
Here before you stands a warrior proud, strong, and true
Of what is yet to come in my life, this is just a preview.

Emotional Blockade

She walks this empty street
Something within her feels incomplete.
What exactly is missing she doesn't know
The void inside her heart has continued to grow.

If she can find answers, perhaps they'll hold the key
Because with all the lies surrounding her, it's hard to see.
Many obstacles have stood in her way
Remaining silent, what she feels she's never been able to say.

All around her people seem so happy and content
Yet she's not even sure for what her life is meant.
As she watches these loving families together, she thinks "I wish that was me"
Seeing how much they care about each other, she feels a hint of jealousy.

In her own life, love was never shown
To her it's an emotion foreign and unknown.
Why her family never wanted her she doesn't understand
Here she is an outcast who was banned.

Their rules she closely followed
Even trying to meet their expectations by sticking to their code.

They must have thought she did something wrong
For they treated her as if she didn't belong.

In their presence, she could've been a ghost
About their kid, you'd never hear them boast.
She knew she was unwanted even at such a young age
Often towards her they directed their rage.

Many nights were spent in tears
Lying awake, she saw all her darkest fears.
She thought of herself as ugly and worthless
The mirror revealed an emotional mess.

Because of her insecurity, she never knew how to let anyone near
Entering adulthood, she still had that nagging fear.
If she allowed anyone close, she was afraid of being betrayed
Not wishing to get hurt again, into the background she let herself fade.

People said they were there for her, but trust didn't come easy
Her fragile, vulnerable side she wouldn't let them see.
Putting up a strong front, those feelings and emotions she locked away
Yet scattered fragments of old memories she saw in her mind each day.

Like a lone wolf she lived a life of solitude

Over the things she went through, though, she'd never brood.
She handled every challenge with dignity and grace
All the while longing for the comfort of a warm, friendly embrace.

Now she finds herself weary from the fight
Very soon day will give way to night.
But she doesn't want to be alone to stumble down this road
She feels herself struggling underneath the weight of her load.

It's time to tear down the walls she's built
Ridding herself of the unnecessary guilt.
A change in her life must be made
Deciding to take a chance on love, she removes the emotional blockade.

These Are The Days

Often in society, we as survivors are misunderstood
People make assumptions on what we've experienced in childhood and adulthood.
Even when we've broken our chains, we still live in silence
Not knowing the real truth, society remains dense.

Untrue myths about abuse and its survivors circulate
False illusions in people's minds they create.
As a result, we're viewed as strange and different
They'd think something else if back to that time and place they were sent.

That we should be over it by now is what we're told
Because on ignorance they are sold.
They figure it was a small portion of our lives so we should have moved on
Little do they know that memories last forever and are never really gone.

Those events did not make up a small part
They left their own effects on our heart.
Down the paths we've been on, others have not tread
Yet they want to tear us down, trying to tell us there's nothing up ahead.

When it comes to the truth about abuse, they live in denial
Those of us who speak out are constantly put on trial.
Every part of our lives they dissect
In a crime committed against us, we become the suspect.

We know it was not our fault and we did nothing wrong
From the wounds we're healing as we try to find where we belong.
With people criticizing us, it is easy to just run
But these challenges we must face for there is much work to be done.

From the world we shouldn't have to hide
If it's one thing they can't take from us it's our pride.
We're the only ones who know what really happened
After all we suffered and endured, our lives didn't end.

For too long our true selves we've concealed
But now it's time for the truth to be revealed.
Emerging from the shadows, we need to break the silence for good
People should know that abuse hurts in childhood and adulthood.

On the dangers of abuse we can help educate
Then maybe we can prevent the hate.
It takes courage to stand strong and true

Isn't it worth it though if we make a difference in the lives of a few.

We shouldn't back down in fear
The chance to make a change is here.
Into this darkness let's shed light
Letting our voices be heard, the truth we'll recite.

Our stories deserve to be told
On our lives other people's opinions should have no hold.
This generation we need to step up and lead
Making our mission about love, not greed.

If we unite together, we are able to be the change the world needs to see
For helping prepare leaders for the next generation of survivors we have the key.
Not only are we survivors, but we're warriors on this battlefield
Standing our ground, these are the days to which silence we won't yield

From Darkness To Light

"Get over it" the most common phrase I always hear
After all I endured, people expect my life to be full of cheer.
They tell me my story is depressing and I should be positive
That the abuse is over and done with is the reason they give.

The truth they don't attempt to find out
They just assume they know what everything is about.
Having selective hearing, they aren't listening to each part
Only seeing the outward appearance, they fail to see straight to the heart.

The heart tells the story that is true and real
Showing hidden emotions we survivors feel.
In our personal battles, we were left alone
For a long time we struggled on our own.

Memories could never fully be erased
With no one there for us, challenges we faced.
Imprinted on our hearts, the emotional scars burned
Every day reminders of the lessons we learned.

As a survivor, I know life isn't always beautiful
Although not our fault, for our abusers' actions we were held responsible.
How much they hurt us they don't really see

Someone else they wanted us to be.

The only way to protect ourselves was if we lied
We covered for them as the truth about hurting us they denied.
Living in silence, we felt we were trapped in a cage
Choosing to take their anger out on us, we became the subject of their rage.

No one came to our rescue
Because what went on behind closed doors they never knew.
The darkness held us prisoner for a while
Somehow we forced ourselves to wear a fake smile.

Once we escaped, different outlets for our pain we tried to find
Hoping the haunting memories we could forever leave behind.
Some of the outlets turned to habits and addictions that hurt us more
For some of us it deepened the pain we felt from before.

A new prison we found ourselves in
One in which we fell prey to our past again.
With our lives spiraling out of control, we began to backslide
Trying to deny what happened to us, we attempted to run and hide.

In running away we didn't get very far
The truth is we cannot deny who we really are.
Our past makes up part of our history
But shining through the not so pretty parts is so much beauty.

We're not using our stories to get people to feel sorry
Our stories show others how strong survivors can be.
Within us a battle we fight
Not giving into evil we stand strong for what is right.

Our lives we chose not to destroy
This new beginning we have we want to enjoy.
We're so much stronger than we give ourselves credit for
Despite the hard times, we believe life holds more.

This journey as a survivor may not always be pleasant
After overcoming obstacles, we know for what our lives are meant.
Even when we faced difficult times, victory we gained
Walking away from the negative, to the past we refused to be chained.

We've been called to help those in need of assistance
Having broken our silence, in their lives we can make a difference.

At one time we found ourselves in their place
Standing beside them, their fears we'll help them face.

Our lives didn't end for we made it out alive
That provides hope for others that they too can survive.
Saving broken hearts, we'll be there for them when day turns to night
As we pave the way, we'll guide them from darkness to light.

Healing Tears

Into this world another special angel was born
Sadly over time her wings would be damaged and torn.
Every one adored this precious gift sent from above
However the ones who should have cherished her showed her no love.

The environment she grew up in was very cold
Many of the things that happened behind closed doors went untold.
A perfectly fine normal American family is how it appeared
Little did people realize that in this household there was much to be feared.

A safe home turned into a violent war zone
With nowhere to go, she faced battles alone.
Nightmares she daily saw and felt were very real
Yet emotions she was forbidden to feel.

Her only friend in the world was her teddy bear
Hugging him, this silent companion seemed to care.
Secrets she carried only he knew
At night, of her tear soaked pillow teddy had the best view.

Time passed by so fast

Having the opportunity to enjoy being a kid didn't last.
With broken wings, she entered into adulthood
Things still weren't all that good.

Memories from those days with her she brought
Struggling because of the flashbacks, she felt distraught.
Yet this angel still managed to smile on the outside
Skillfully her fragile, vulnerable parts she would hide.

What she was dealing with no one was aware
Her laughter and gentle nature covered the despair.
She knew better than to let anyone past the walls she worked hard to build
Contents of her life story she wasn't ready to have spilled.

People didn't seem to notice that at times she grew distant
In their own lives they were too caught up in the moment.
The strong one in life she always remained
Helping others, about her problems she never complained.

Unlike others, she had no place she could call home
Going from one place to another her life consisted of being on the roam.

Although she was starting over, the pieces didn't seem complete
A sense of loneliness settled in as she approached the brink of defeat.

To everyone else around her she was a hero
Credit they gave her she thought she fell below.
She'd made it her personal mission to aid those in need
However, from emotional wounds, her own heart had begun to bleed.

After all these years she still didn't let her true feelings show
The fake belief that crying was weakness she continued to follow.
Holding it all in, she feared she would break
This smile she wore she could no longer fake.

Picking up her teddy bear, she hugged him tight
Giving way to her emotions, she surrendered the fight.
As she released her feelings, the walls were pushed aside
She found the missing piece when the healing tears she cried

For All The Survivors

What's the purpose of life you ask
Most of it you've been forced to hide behind a mask.
Your deepest secrets go untold
They remain buried as the information you with hold.

You fight alone on this vast battlefield
Watching others as to society's rules they yield.
Their morals and values they willingly compromise
Trading themselves in, they become blinded by the lies.

Because you're different, you get cast to the side
By your own guidelines you choose to abide.
The truth you refused to deny
Unveiling it, society's rules you decided to defy.

For years the painful memories you concealed
Knowing that harsh judgment you'd receive if your story you revealed.
People put in their two cents while picking you apart
They figured they held all the answers to the emotions of your heart.

Tired of false assumptions, you kept silent
Thinking that the details of your past didn't matter and weren't relevant.

Disappearing, you blended into the background
You maintained your distance, not wanting to be found.

Others gained attention and popularity by stepping into the spotlight
Working quietly behind the scenes, you hid out of sight.
Your efforts didn't entirely go unnoticed
The effects of your hard work were witnessed.

Every day your voice does matter
To those in need, your message is a valuable treasure.
You may think people only see you as broken and fragile
Yet there are many out there who find you strong and beautiful.

Your story deserves to be told
When others hear it, onto hope they grab hold.
They look at all the obstacles you've had to overcome
Suddenly they have faith that into a strong survivor they too can blossom.

You shouldn't have to hide or live your life in denial
What happened wasn't your fault and you broke the cycle.
No matter what your history is, it's something you don't have to repeat
You can rebuild a life that is new and

complete.

The myths society believes about survivors we need to remove
That they are false we need to prove.
Speaking out, we're able to make a difference
As we step out from the shadows, let them feel our presence.

If we want to make a change, there's much work to be finished
Just because we suffered in our past doesn't mean we perished.
From the darkness we emerged stronger than before
Lost hope and faith we're given a chance to restore.

From our stories others will be inspired
Our determination, courage, and voices are required.
It's time the truth be heard
Standing together, we won't be beaten or battered.

For us better days wait
To begin writing a new sequel it's not too late.
The violence that shatters innocent lives we can help end
An insight we have since to us it happened.

Let's make this world a safer place
Abuse is something no one should have to face.

It's our mission to save those lives before its too late
Because no one deserves to suffer such a cruel fate.

Way Back When

Looking back on my life I've seen how much I've grown
Back then though, I struggled through tough times on my own.
It was a different story when I started out
I had no idea what my life would turn out to be about.

Growing up, I was this kid who was always scared
To everyone else I constantly got compared.
My parents really didn't take much time to be around
Staying to myself, I blended in with the background.

In my broken home, love was never expressed
Emotions and feelings were always repressed.
As a kid, I witnessed so much anger and hate
Often I wondered what would be my fate.

Hearing negative remarks, I felt the sting of rejection
From the abuse I had no protection.
In my life they absolutely showed no interest
With all the violence at home, I couldn't stay focused.

Having no place to go, I only had myself to depend on
Controlling my life, I became their pawn.

I watched my dreams and goals slip out of sight
Soon I struggled to even see the light.

After I left, I still lived in denial
Not wanting to own up to the abuse that was hurtful.
For a while I didn't want to admit that what happened was real
So I still had yet to allow myself to begin to heal.

To block out memories, I used methods that were self-destructive
The more I tried to cover the pain, the more I lost my will to live.
Everything about my life I questioned
Under all the strain I felt burdened.

Attempting to run away, my problems I refused to face
I thought if I told my story people would see me as a disgrace.
Deep inside, I knew I couldn't continue traveling down this road
Because to a dead end it would lead if I followed.

Making the decision to let myself heal, I got my life on track
The first step I took was taking my life back.
On the areas I needed healing I concentrated
My life I learned not to take for granted.

Even now, I am still discovering my voice
But speaking out has been for me the best choice.
Everything in my life I didn't lose
Following my heart, I stand strong in my views and values.

There are days that within myself a battle I fight
Believing in myself, though, I know it will be all right.
No more do I hide behind my fear
I've broken my silence and now my voice I want others to hear.

From victim to survivor, I made a major breakthrough
Although I've come a long way, I have more growing to do.
After losing myself for so long, I'm learning to love myself again
Because I know I'm not the same girl from way back when.

Unspoken Thoughts

So many thoughts of mine have gone unsaid
I still struggle with anger issues after the childhood I led.
The events from back then I don't quite understand
All I know is that being a kid definitely wasn't grand.

Every time you looked at me, I could sense the resentment
Under the ice-cold exterior, I wondered where the love went.
Always in your presence strong I tried to appear
Since you said crying was weakness, I shed not one tear.

My own mom I watched you shatter apart
Even though she'd never say it, I know you broke her heart.
You finally wore her down completely under your control
Often I intervened so she wouldn't have to play the victim role.

All those years I wish she would have had the strength to leave you
Because she never deserved the hell you put her through.
Each night I listened to her cry
I could tell she had begun to emotionally die.

To us you became an unrecognizable stranger
Your unresolved issues placed our lives in danger.
By your anger you were totally consumed
If I failed to meet your expectations, you fumed.

For a while you were the person I feared the most
I found that it was better to stay invisible like a ghost.
Besides the physical abuse, I took your emotional abuse as well
Threatened into silence, I had no one to tell.

I wish I could say that things are now perfect
But from the abuse I still feel every lasting effect.
In time the scars have started to fade
For my freedom, though, so much I had to trade.

I lived a long time in denial
Not wanting to admit that my childhood was a painful trial.
I didn't want to own up to what happened
With all the memories haunting me, it was hard to pretend.

When I thought about what you did, I felt so much rage inside
Because of you, my emotions and feelings I had to hide.
I've battled with trust and abandonment issues

from a father who hurt me
Due to your brainwashing, the good in me it's taken awhile for me to see.

As difficult as it was, you I learned to forgive
Letting go of the hate is the only way I can truly live.
How you could hurt your family I'll never know
I do know I won't be like you and your abusive traits I won't show.

In my life I made my choice
I choose to expose the truth by using my voice.
No, the things you put me through I'll never forget
A fighter and survivor, I've shown strength to overcome challenges I met.

Many more obstacles I will have to face
The possibility of a better life I embrace.
How not to be in my own life is the greatest lesson you taught
Saying farewell to the past, it's healing for myself that I've sought.

Time To Go My Own Way

It's taken me awhile to see things won't ever be the same
There's no reason to stay when on me you always put the blame.
I've held on for way too long
Now I know that for you I can't continue to be strong.

I can't go back and change how things were
Neither can I erase all the pain I had to weather.
The only regret I have is that I didn't see it long ago
But it's not worth living my life hiding in a shadow.

What else is left to say other than I tried
Pushing myself to be everything you wanted, I nearly died.
The person I am though I shouldn't have to sacrifice
Now as I stand here, I am finally taking my own advice.

I loved you with all I had to love
Yet in your eyes I fell short of being an angel sent from above.
Every time you walked away I felt the rejection
All I ever wanted was your love and affection.

I thought I could fix that which had been broken

Sadly to the truth I awoken.
You refused to put aside differences and compromise
That you weren't willing to let go of the past I began to realize.

I used to wonder where I went wrong
Thinking it was my fault all along.
Those were the lies you wanted me to believe
If you kept me in the dark, great things I wouldn't achieve.

Try to cover up your life, but you are transparent
Justifying your behavior, on me you pass judgment.
In your mind, you still see me as a failure
To your needs though I no longer cater.

Maybe one day you'll see what you missed before it's too late
As for me, my life choices I don't have to contemplate.
I just can't let you hold me back anymore
Because by dwelling on the past, I'll never find my open door.

I guess sometimes you aren't able to make it right
Especially when the other person won't put up a fight.
Only so much could I do on my part
Until I eventually came to terms that with you there wouldn't be a new start

So this life of pain and drama I'm leaving behind
Sometimes you have to say goodbye in order for your way to find.
I never wanted it to turn out like this
The caring person I knew once upon a time ago I dearly miss.

I'd rather leave now then find myself at the point of no return
Not looking back, this bridge I shall burn.
Listening to my heart instead of my head, a leap of faith I take
No more living a life that is fake.

It's time for me to discover the girl within
Victory from the pain I know I can win.
Let it dawn a brand new day
In this world it's time for me to go my own way.

Sisters In The Fight

On different paths in life we each travel
A quest to reveal the truth provides our fuel.
We've embarked upon our own healing journey
For the things that we saw and felt others did not see.

Our stories are certainly not the same
Yet from our pain, we could all feel the shame.
Darkness surrounded us day and night
Often we wondered if we'd ever find the light.

None of us thought about what others were going through
We were focused on the abuse in our own lives that we knew.
Escaping our prison became our only concern
Who had it worse than us we didn't have time to discern.

The truth is our stories can never be compared
Because we each suffered pain from the horrors we fared.
What right do we have to tell someone they didn't have it as bad
We may all be survivors, but each of our tales are sad.

That we made it out alive we should be glad
But we shouldn't make being a survivor some sort of fad.
Telling others how they need to heal is not our

place
Their own methods let them find and embrace.

Survival is not a competition of who had it worse
The common goal we share is the desire to end this curse.
In all kinds of ways we can each make a difference
So let's put away the condemnation and remove the defense.

It's not about who's doing more
What's important is we find our open door.
Our anger from our pain we should not take out on anyone
Because then we are no better than those who hurt us, making our lives not so fun.

That we're all survivors is our common link
Then why do we allow one another to sink?
No, we're not the same people, but we have the same goal
We want to start a change that will help heal the soul.

Isn't it enough that from the rest of the world our emotions we put aside
From our fellow survivors we shouldn't need to hide.
We don't like others judging us on our past
Let's not do that to each other but create a bond that will last.

There's a world out there crying out in need
How can we save them if we're engrossed and self absorbed in greed.
Each time we tear one another down, more time we waste
We're here to help and reach out, not to criticize and chaste.

On this battlefield we cannot fight alone
We must work together so back together these broken hearts can be sewn.
With open minds, we have to look at the picture overall
Standing together, let's not cause other survivors to fall.

We are who we are
However, we can help others get far.
Side by side, into the darkness we're able to shine our light
When it comes down to it, the connecting thread is that we're all sisters in the fight.

The Most Precious Gift

I found myself thinking about the greatest gift
one could find
Then your name just happened to enter my
mind.
In my life you are the angel sent from above
Showing me the real meaning of love.

Thinking about you, a smile crossed my face
You've touched my heart in many ways with
your beauty and grace.
At one point I was close to the brink of defeat
But by chance we had the opportunity to meet.

I can't even begin to tell you how much you've
made a difference
There is light and hope in your very presence.
Do you realize how many you inspire
With a compassionate heart, of helping others
you never tire.

Broken wings you know how to heal
Your emotions you're not afraid to feel.
Imperfection in others is something you don't
see
Looking beyond, you focus on the inner
beauty.

Caring and understanding, you refuse to judge
based on the past
Instead you work to give hope that people
have a future that can last.
When it comes down to it, you're willing to

make self-sacrifices
Always standing steadfast, you won't back
down to peer pressure that entices.

You give people something to believe in
Sending the message that victory in their lives
they can win.
Because of you faith once lost gets restored
Is it any wonder by so many you're adored.

Honor and courage through your veins flow
It's determination and strength that in your
story show.
Your values you hold close to your heart
Nothing can tear your virtues apart.

To the suffering that goes on you are not blind
Ways to put back the broken pieces you find.
On your own mission of mercy you ask for
nothing in return
From you lessons to never give up we can
learn.

With love you replace the hate
Taking people's hands, you walk with them
through destiny's gate.
You're the comforter in times of sorrow
The guardian angel that helps trapped souls
face tomorrow.

Your compassionate nature has no boundaries
Many hurting hearts your love frees.
Expectations for others you don't hold
Gently you bring you the stories in people that

have gone untold.

In my life you are truly a hero
You've taught me things I didn't know.
Just like a rose our friendship continues to grow and bloom
Deep within my heart for you there will always be room.

So many reasons why I admire and respect you I could give
Perhaps the most important is you gave me a reason to live.
For the best gift I could keep searching the world through and through
But I all ready found the most precious gift and it's you.

Can You Hear Me

She lives her life from day to day
In one place too long she doesn't stay.
Home is not where her heart lies
Forced to make it on her own, she severed the ties.

Not much of her background does she reveal
She figures that to people her story wouldn't appeal.
The less they know the better
From her past she's all ready wearing a scarlet letter.

Avoiding eye contact, she always looks away
Because if asked about herself, she wouldn't know what to say.
Behind a mask, she covers up her fragile side
She's trying to salvage what's left of her pride.

Most of her life she's been told what to do and how to act
Even hearing about the qualities that as a person she lacked.
Pulled in every direction, she was expected to comply
Her own life back she couldn't buy.

People snubbed her for being different
To them though the truth was transparent.
Remarks she heard ware cruel and insensitive
It was tough enough that in a violent home she had to live.

To the life of an outcast she learned to adapt
Between controlling parents and peer abuse,
her life was mapped.
In silence the emotional pain she suffered
Her voice continued to go unheard.

A fairytale life she didn't experience
That she lived in a happy, loving family was a
false pretense.
Dreams she had were daily shattered
All she knew was how it felt to be physically
and emotionally battered.

Every night she wondered if she even had a
future
Especially when so many tears replaced
laughter.
Finding freedom became her main goal
She longed for the day when once again she
would feel whole.

Now she faces the world on her own
Yet for others' actions she still has to atone.
In places her heart is still broken
There are scars that remain from way back
then.

Sitting by herself, she watches people pass her
by
They don't seem to notice her as she lets out a
sigh.
Just like before she's invisible to the world
around

Feeling unwanted, she wonders if there's a place where love and hope abound.

She desperately wants to tell someone what she's been through
But after years of locking it inside, it's hard to know what to do.
The issues in her life she can't continue to ignore
There has to be a way to heal and move on to something more.

Taking the first step forward, her efforts get thwarted
Not listening to her, people leave her stranded.
Judgmental, on her a cold shoulder they turn
Her side of the story they don't bother to learn.

Adversity she meets as her story she tries to tell
Once again she finds herself crawling back into a shell.
The last thing she needs is more drama
She's all ready endured so much trauma.

Looking out over the water, she screams silently inside
How much longer will this pain she have to hide.
What people don't know or understand they seem to fear
Making their assumptions, the truth they don't hear.

A stranger walks by but stops in his tracks
Recognizing him as one of her peers from
work, she braces for verbal attacks.
Instead, he looks deep into her eyes
Past the scars, he sees the beauty that
underneath lies.

He hears her heart's silent cry calling "Can you
hear me"
Knowing she's been hurt in life, he only wants
her to be happy.
"I can hear you," is the only phrase he speaks
Releasing emotional tears, comfort in his
presence she seeks.

I Am.....

I am a person with a story to tell
Finally ready to be heard after suffering years of hell.
For so long I've lived in silence as I hid behind a mask
Now I know it's time for me to carry on a new task.

I am a phoenix rising above the ashes of my past
Focusing instead on having a future that can last.
Chances and risks I won't be afraid to take
Not repeating the history of before, I have a new life to make.

I am a dreamer holding onto my goals
From victim to survivor, I changed roles.
In myself and my dreams I continue to believe
As I reach for the stars, there's nothing I can't achieve.

I am a fearless traveler following my heart
With a leap of faith, I'm out to get another start.
My hope helps to guide the way
Saying farewell to the past, I move on to a brand new day.

I am the author of my life's story
Writing a better sequel about me.
The previous chapters I can't erase

Closing them, though, new pages I write as
new adventures I embrace.

I am an advocate for what is right
Looking for justice, the truth I bring into the
light.
I refuse to back down in the midst of adversity
The damages abuse causes people need to see.

I am a voice for the victims and survivors who
haven't been able to speak
Being able to survive the pain of the past
makes us strong, not weak.
True beauty lies beneath the scars we bear
To find the courage and strength that we
possess is rare.

I am a guardian angel for those in need
Through the dark times, I help to guide and
lead.
Their hearts' cries I can hear
Comforting and protecting, I calm their fear.

I am a warrior on life's battlefield
Knowing not the meaning of defeat, to the
enemy I don't yield.
I stand beside my sisters and brothers in the
fight
Together, for those trapped in silence, we'll
shine our light.

I am an eagle soaring to a greater height
Allowing my wings to heal, I'm ready for
flight.

Beyond the horizon, opportunities wait
To get to live the life I've always wanted it's never too late.

I am a passionate soul speaking out
My ability to create change I don't doubt.
It's my desire to make a difference by giving back
Spreading love as hate I attack.

Most of all, I am a fighter and survivor still standing strong
Finally finding exactly where I belong.
Taking my life back, I now have control
It is with pride and honor that I wear the title Survivor and play the role.

The Girl Within

On the surface I appear to be strong
As if I know exactly where I belong.
People look at me, seeing only what's on the outside
Yet there's so much ore to e on the inside that I hide.

The fragile parts of me I don't always show
I guess the real me it's time for people to know.
Honestly, I am just a girl still fighting to survive
Never taking my life for granted, I consider myself blessed to be alive.

I've witnessed terrible things I wish I wouldn't have seen
Fighting on my own, I had no one on which I could lean.
Throughout my childhood and marriage to the pain of abuse I was exposed
Forced to remain silent, the information was never disclosed.

Into the darkest times of my life I plunged
To the battle of life and death I found myself challenged.
Through physical pain the emotional pain I relieved
Having lost my faith, I watched dreams slip away that I could have achieved.

Within myself I felt empty and hollow
A destructive road I began to follow.
My idea of freedom from the pain was to end it all
Standing on the edge of my life, I braced myself to take the fall.

Not knowing love in my life, I felt I had nothing to live for
Wanting to escape, I thought this was the open door.
Yet deep inside I knew I really didn't want to die
I just couldn't continue to live a lie.

The first step I took was to rid myself of hate
Love for the girl within I had to create.
That also meant learning to forgive those who hurt me
Otherwise the good qualities in my heart my anger wouldn't let me see.

Next, a chance I decided to take on speaking out
This was the only way to start to erase the self-doubt.
Using courage and strength, my silence I shattered
Finally sharing my story of the years I was battered.

The best decision I made was to use my voice
Even though at times it can be tough, I don't regret this choice.

I admit there are still some insecurities left behind
But not by who I once was but by who I am now I want to be defined.

Everyday these broken wings continue to heal
The truth about my past I'm not afraid to reveal.
At times I do question what my life is about
Feeling I'm not going anywhere and just stuck in a drought.

From the abuse of my past I still battle anger and rage
So I use writing as my outlet rather then going on a rampage.
When it comes to relationships and dating, I hold back and hesitate
Afraid of being hurt like before, I don't want to be trapped in another abusive fate.

I do have many trust issues
Having been betrayed by those who didn't understand or share my views.
It's hard for me to let people get too near
That they'll judge me on my past and walk away is my fear.

After living a life of abuse I know these things are normal to feel
A part of me is searching for a life that is real.
On this journey of healing, new things about myself I'm discovering
However, my scars I'm not covering.

The scars are a reminder of how far I've made it
Other survivors and victims my story can help benefit.
I won't be afraid of the unknown anymore
As a survivor I have more growing to do but I'm not the victim from before.

Many lessons I have learned along the way
Most importantly, I am proud of the woman I am today.
There are areas in my life I need to work on
But I'll keep on loving the girl within, not letting her fade until she's gone.

Survivor's Healing Creed

I believe that the past made me the strong person I am today.

I believe that it is more than okay to release my feelings and emotions.

I believe crying is a sign of strength, not a sign of weakness.

I believe age has no part to play in making a difference because one is never too old and never too young to change the world.

I believe it's normal to feel anger from the abuse I suffered, but I must control the anger and not let it control me.

I believe that I don't have to repeat the history of my abusers but I have the power in me to break the cycle, refusing to be like them.

I believe my scars are a beautiful testimony of my survival.

I believe that the after effects left behind are challenges in my life I must fight to overcome but that doesn't mean I am a victim.

I believe in a life after abuse for it's never too late to get the life I've always wanted when life gives me a second chance.

I believe that I will never forget what I went through but it is my choice whether I choose to forgive those who hurt me.

I believe there's no right or wrong way to heal and I'm the only one who knows what will help me to heal.

I believe it is important to surround myself with positive people so I can continue to grow as a person.

I believe that my self-perspective is what allows me to transform from the victim of yesterday into the survivor of today.

I believe it's important to love myself so that I learn to accept myself and can reach out to others even more, showing them love.

I believe that risks and chances are worth taking, otherwise I'll never know what I could be or where my life could go.

I believe every opportunity I get in life I should seize because once those moments pass by, I can't get them back.

I believe that just because I've been in an abusive relationship or marriage before doesn't mean I won't find real, true love eventually.

I believe it isn't right or fair to compare my story with someone else's because everyone's story is different and since I wasn't there I have no right to judge them or tell them I had it worse.

I believe that when I write or tell my story, it doesn't mean I am dwelling on the past but means I'm expressing feelings I kept locked inside for years.

I believe I should never use my experiences as a way to gain pity and sympathy but use it as something positive to give others hope and show the world how strong survivors are.

I believe that my story is just as important as anyone else's.

I believe it doesn't matter how long I endured abuse, I still feel the pain from it was greatly affected by it.

I believe helping others shouldn't be a competition because it isn't about who does the most work; it's about who cares enough to make self sacrifices to help save lives, doing it not for popularity or fame but because they have a desire and passion to do so.

I believe people shouldn't feel sorry or pity me for what I went through but be happy for me that I have lived and survived to tell my story.

I believe that not every survivor is ready to share their story with the world but for those of us who are, we should be a voice for them.

I believe older survivors shouldn't act superior to the younger ones; instead they should help them so in return they will be prepared to lead the next generation.

I believe that no matter our age or our backgrounds, we can all learn from one another.

I believe it takes teamwork to spread awareness, prevent abuse, and make this world a better place.

I believe my inner child needs to be nurtured, loved, and cared for.

I believe every story deserves to be told and every voice deserves to be heard.

I believe that while the early chapters of my life have all ready been written, I can write new pages for a better sequel.

I believe that even though I grew up in a broken home and came from a rough background, it doesn't mean I can't have a happily ever after in life.

I believe dreams and goals are important to have because they give me something to live

for, providing me with hope to keep holding on.
I believe lessons I've learned from the past are stepping-stones to creating a brighter future since I know what not to do.

I believe the healing process takes one day at a time, one step at a time and should not be rushed.

I believe the most precious gifts to give other survivors and victims are love, compassion, care, understanding, hope, faith, encouragement, inspiration, motivation, and happiness.

I believe that we can all be leaders if we are willing to step up and speak out.

I believe survivors are the most beautiful people there are who have so much courage, strength and determination inside them.

I believe that I am defined by who I am today and shouldn't be judged on who I was in my past.

I believe that every voice matters!

I believe that we can pick up where the leaders of the past left off and continue to follow their vision as we work to carry out our own missions and purposes in life.

I believe that when I believe in myself, I can achieve anything

HOPE Acronym

Holding

Onto

Possibilities

Everyday

Worth Waiting For

A picture of a happy smiling couple hangs on the wall
Looking at it though, terrible memories she starts to recall.
The man beside her was someone of whom she was afraid
In the end, her love and trust he betrayed.

It's been some time since she walked away
Still, the events from that marriage stay with her each day.
Instead of being in a loving relationship, she found herself in a boxing match
From the man she loved anger and violence began to hatch.

Emotional and physical abuse she suffered at his hand
Bruises made it hard for her to stand.
Putting her down with cruel words, her spirit he broke
He'd follow her, as a reaction from her he hoped to evoke.

Their vows he never held to or even meant
The day they were wed to an emotional prison she'd be sent.
For a while she stayed wanting things to go back to how they were before
Soon she realized she'd never be the apple of his eye that he'd adore.

Making the decision to leave, she left it all behind
A life free from abuse she set out to find.
With a broken heart, those chapters of her life she had to close
Between living a lie and her own safety she chose.

At first she questioned if the choice she made was right
Then she remembered how rather than fighting for her with her he'd fight.
She knows it's better going it alone
Rather than be with someone who every part of her life tried to own.

Yet at times she finds it hard to believe the love they once had is gone
Even starting over, the hurt and pain linger on.
She wonders how it got to the point where everything fell apart
Now she's left to put together the pieces of her scarred heart.

She knows it isn't her fault even though on her he placed the blame
Refusing to hate him, she accepts nothing will ever be the same.
Letting go, she's found inner peace in saying good-bye
Because she couldn't continue living this lie.

All around her she sees couples so happy and

in love
Part of her longs to know what it's like to be someone's angel sent from above.
Her friends have that special someone that of them can't get enough
Playing third wheel and hearing about their dates constantly is tough.

Everyone tells her she should get out and date
Acting as if being single is some terrible fate.
In her heart, she knows she needs time to heal
Until she allows herself to heal, she won't be able to have love that's real.

Being single isn't something bad
If anything, it's let her see qualities in herself she never knew she had.
Dreams and goals she put on hold she has a chance to achieve
Right now, what matters most is the love from friends and family that she gets to receive.

She hasn't given up on finding true love one day
A little bit scared of falling in love, she knows there's someone out there who will love and cherish her in every single way.
But wanting it to happen on its own, she doesn't go looking for love anymore
When it comes to her, it will be the most beautiful, precious gift worth waiting for.

More Than Meets The Eye

Behind your smile, you hide the pain so well
Locked up are secrets that you would never tell.
Your heart has been broken into so many pieces
Hiding it, you wonder if the hurting ever ceases.

Some wounds can't be healed with Neosporin and a band-aid
Still running deep are scars that the events from the past made.
They're visible to you even when them you try to conceal
People will judge you on your past if anything you reveal.

It's all about keeping up a good appearance
If you let your guard down, others throw in their two cents.
There are times it's easier to remain silent
Then the truth by people can't be bent.

That they'll regard you as nothing more than fragile is what you fear
Because they tend to hear only what they want to hear.
But ignorance gives them a distorted view
They'd see someone amazing if they saw you

the way that I do.

Anyone who doesn't get to know the real you loses out
You're beautiful inside and out and this I know without a doubt.
Others may focus on flaws but in you I find a priceless treasure
Never once have you given up after all you've had to endure.

Not very many people would have had the will to go on
Yet here you are standing strong when all you once knew is now gone.
The negatives you made into something positive
Sending out a message that a better life others can live.

When things fell apart, your life you chose to rebuild
A true warrior, you continued fighting on life's battlefield.
You never allowed anything to hold you back
Going for your dreams, you proved strength you don't lack.

I understand what you've been through
Just know that I won't ever think any less of you.
Even when you face hard times, you always find a way
The silver lining to every cloud you look for in

each new day.

Refusing to follow the crowd, you never take the bait
Instead achieving your goals, you don't sit around and wait.
You're never afraid to stand up for what you believe in
Reaching out to others, you help them to win.

Saving lives is what you do best
The truth you shed light on even if put to the test.
Every obstacle you and challenge you rise above
Always showing how tough you are when push comes to shove.

The definition of a fighter and survivor you fit
Never did you let the fire burn out once in your heart it was lit.
Looking at you, those scars completely fade
In my eyes, you're someone beautifully made.

I'm proud of you for making it this far
To me you stand out with all your qualities and my vision of you hasn't begun to mar.
If people try to tell you that you're worthless, it's a huge lie
Because trust me, there's more to you than meets the eye.

Through The Years

A picture is worth a thousand words is what they say
But down memory lane a picture also paves the way.
I came across one of you while cleaning out my past
Finding it amazing how time can fly by so fast.

Just seeing your face again brought back memories of days long gone
Yet somehow over the passing years they've lingered on.
You've been missing from my life for quite some time
However, I'll never forget how against me you committed an abusive crime.

Back then it was only my flaws and imperfections you'd see
Here it is years later and you still don't know the real me.
Oh, I very well know I haven't turned out the way you expected
Then again, what you put me through nobody ever suspected.

In many ways my life has changed
The events of the past for myself I wouldn't have arranged.

Things happened that I never planned for
Isn't it surprising though how speaking out can open another door?
All this time you assumed I would keep silent
Hoping I'd cover for you so the truth would be bent.
Since you don't know me, you aren't aware of the strength I have inside
Now that I took back control of my life, from you I won't hide.

As tragic as it was, the past helped transform me into who I am today
Breaking my silence, there's so much I can now say.
This isn't retribution or payback
More like on this battlefield of life it's my method of attack.

When I left, I realized I wasn't the only one out there
All around me were survivors everywhere.
They too had experienced their own pain
Uniting together, strength in numbers they started to gain.

From victim to survivor, a new role I played
Joining with others, I saw in them the courage they displayed.
So many compassionate souls stand with one another in this fight
Reaching out to rescue those lost, there's never been a more beautiful sight.

Knowing I'm not alone, my story I want others to hear
Not taking a chance is the only thing I should fear
I found the place where I belong
Finding my passion in life and doing what I love, I can't go wrong.

I'm so much stronger than you know
A testimony of survival the scars you left behind show.
Maybe this isn't the person you want me to be
But I am happy with who I've become, knowing I'm now free.

Even without your guidance, I turned out all right
It was always my dream to help others in the fight.
I walked away from a past full of violence and hate
Hoping that my own legacy I could create.

My heart continues to lead me down the right road
Dreams and goals I had put on hold I'm glad I followed.
Something negative I made positive
Through the years, I will still spread the word that an abuse free life is possible to live.

Traits of a Survivor

Rises above the ashes of the past

Perseveres through life's storms

Compassionate towards other survivors and victims

Reaches out a hand to help those in need

Insight provides understanding to what others have gone through

Uses past experiences to pave the way for others to speak out

Spreads awareness by shedding light on the truth

Looks for the open doors in life

Determined to rebuild a life that is abuse free

Gives hope to others when sharing own story

Encourages victims and survivors in their journey of healing

Guides those who are lost and alone

Teaches fellow survivors to fly again

Soars to new heights
Believes in goals and dreams

Unites with other warriors to fight for all who are trapped

Courage to take a stand for what is right

Takes a step forward to lead those still wandering

Hears the voices of the unheard

Sees the feelings and emotions of others by looking into their hearts

Works behind the scenes to help others heal

Seizes opportunities to make a difference in life

Chooses to be the change needed in the world

Listens to what people have to say, not fixating on just one part of the story

Builds a bright future from the broken pieces of the past

Writes a new and better sequel to the chapters all ready written

Explores beyond the horizons, discovering the

destination waiting

Knows no limits when achieving goals
Fights for the rights of those who haven't been granted justice

Dispels myths about abuse by speaking the truth

Doesn't pass judgment on anyone

Shelters and comforts ones hurting and grieving

Never afraid to show emotions and feelings

Leaves no fellow survivor or victim behind on life's battlefield

Passes on knowledge about dangers and effects of abuse to those who haven't been abused

Strives to eliminate the stigmas surrounding survivors and victims

Gives without expecting anything in return

Embraces possibilities life offers

Opens the eyes to those blinded by ignorance to what goes on in the lives of abuse victims and survivors

Takes action instead of just talking about achievements hoped to be accomplished

Understands that everyone's situation is different so they heal in their own way

Overcomes obstacles and tears down walls blocking the way

Shows the world what love is about by replacing and removing hate in own life

Views reflection of one who is a survivor and no longer a victim

Breaks the chains of the past in order to move on to a new day and have the life they always wanted to live

Reflects on how much growing has been done through the years, from where they once were to where they are today

Loves and accepts every part of themselves

Lives in the present, making the most of each moment

Has faith in own abilities

Puts together pieces of their life's puzzle to see how beautiful it is and can be

Never quits or backs down during hard times

Envisions what can be, not what could have been
Pushes onward rather then stay stuck in the past

Keeps holding on, knowing the present and future don't have to repeat the history from before

My Wish For The World

Everyone has their own wishes they hope to see come true
Because in their lives people want a chance at something new.
I thought about the dreams I carry in my heart
Realizing they're not about me but helping others get a fresh start.

When people ask me what I want my reply is that with my life I'm content
To make a difference in this world is the reason I was sent.
Here's my list of wishes to see the world become a better place
It is my goal that every opportunity I get to create a change I'll embrace.

I wish that all children grew up in homes surrounded by love
That parents would cherish and protect these little angels from above.
Kids should be treasured for they make the world a brighter place
They shouldn't have to grow up too fast and a life of neglect and abuse face.

I wish people would see the beauty they have

inside
Instead of feeling that who they really are they must hide.
Everyone is unique and special in their own way
But they'll never know that if they only hear negative remarks others say.

I wish women would know for real love it's okay to wait
Being single is a gift, not some horrible fate.
Never feel you need a man to be happy and complete
Let love happen on its own for it will be more precious when the right one you meet.

I wish people wouldn't judge others based on their past
If they only got to know the person they might find a friendship that could last.
One shouldn't be dismissed because of what happened before
What matters is they moved on and closed that door.

I wish that in their dreams people would continue to believe
Knowing with hope and faith anything they could achieve.
Dreams give us a reason to hold on
It's when they're taken away that a part of us feels gone.

I wish there was no abuse so innocent lives

wouldn't be shattered
Too many women, men, and children from violence are left battered.
Home should be a safe shelter to go
Not some war zone where pain is the only thing families know.

I wish pain and suffering world wide would be relieved
That people would lend a hand so help for those in need could be received.
If we all just took the time to reach out, a difference we'd make
For it is better to give back rather than just take.

I wish every voice was heard
Ignorance blinds people to the truth so they think it's absurd.
So many stories go untold
By listening, you can save someone and on life they won't lose hold.

I wish that towards each other people would show more compassion
With understanding, a burden you could help lighten.
Others need to know that in what they go through they are not alone
We have a chance to be there for them as we let that be known.

I wish there wasn't any malice or hate
If we just set aside our differences, maybe to

one another we could relate.
How many hearts will be torn apart
Before working together to spread love and peace we begin to start.
I wish there were more who would speak out
Finding strength within, they'd overcome all self-doubt.
To start change, we must stand steadfast for what is right
On the truth we are the ones who can shed light.

So those are the things I wish to come true
When we fight for each other, we have the power to make a breakthrough.
Let's work together to help a world in need
A world filled with love, faith, hope, and peace has an opportunity to blossom if we plant that seed.

One More Day

I had a dream in which I revisited my past
It was as if into another time and place I'd been cast.
In the dream a guide appeared to me
He said, "You're here because there are things you need to see."

Taking my hand, he led me down that old familiar road
Without saying a word, down memory lane I followed.
I couldn't help but wonder what I was doing here
But curiosity soon overcame all fear.

The first stop was my childhood
Watching scenes play out, in silence I stood.
A picture of a happy family came into view
For a moment I wondered if this could be true.

They just seemed so content
Nothing like it was in the present.
Laughter and joy actually filled the household
The atmosphere revealed no traces of somewhere cold.

From holidays to sporting events, everything

was a joyous occasion
Being together for them was reason enough for celebration.
I had forgotten about the good times we once shared
That at one point in time I'd been a happy little girl whose parents cared.

Then those scenes faded out of sight
The friendly, loving home turned into one filled with fright.
Shouting and yelling broke out, floating through the air
The events unfolding still gave me a scare.

Off to the side sat the little girl in tears
Holding her teddy bear close, she felt new fears.
Her parents continued to fight
As the father made the mother feel she could do nothing right.

To protect her mother, she tried to intervene
Then she became the one caught in between.
All too soon she had to grow up fast
Her innocent childhood never had a chance to last.

Next came the years in which her mom became deeply depressed
The more she withdrew, the more it progressed.
Her mom was nothing but a shadow of her former self

Sounds of crying from the closed doors told
her heart had been put away on a shelf.

School was anything but fun
The target of bullies, her they would threaten.
Now a teen, many challenges she faced
Between school and home, her grades slipped
as the usual As and Bs were erased.

I watched as this lost teen ran away to a secret
place
There her real feelings and emotions she could
embrace.
Looking out over the water, she wondered
what lay on the other side
Maybe someday she'd be free where she
wouldn't have to hide.

Turning the pages, we ventured onto the
second part
Here the teen, now a woman, struggled with a
broken heart.
From her childhood, she carried the pain left
behind
Involved in a life of drinking and cutting, her
way she couldn't find.

In all the wrong places she went looking for
love
Losing self-respect since no guy treated her
like an angel from above.
Time after time they threw her away
Only looking for a good time, they never did
stay.

She eventually met a guy and they married
Yet he had secrets of his own that he buried.
Happily ever after became a nightmare surrounded by hate
Marital bliss transformed into a cruel, violent fate.

Once again she was a victim trapped in silence
Constantly she fought back in self-defense.
He took her spirit and tore it down
How he enjoyed making her cry and see her frown.

I braced myself for what was about to appear
Knowing the darkest times were near.
I saw her locked in the bathroom, contemplating whether to go on
Hurting herself again, her hope and faith were almost gone.

I felt the tears well in my eyes as she wanted to give in
Oh how I wanted to tell her to hang on and that she could win.
Her life was spiraling out of control and hanging by a delicate thread
The thought racing through her mind was I wish I was dead.

"Why are you showing me this?" I asked my guide
"So I can show you this," he said, "so hold on for the ride."

Flashing forward, a different me came into view
There stood a woman who knew her real value.

Her reflection was of a beautiful survivor
One on the way to becoming a thriver.
Confidence and courage flowed through her heart
She'd taken a chance to have a new start.

Gone were the signs of the lonely, lost girl of before
Here was a woman who found her open door.
Negative circumstances she made into something positive
Not giving up, she knew she had a reason to live.

"I don't understand though, there was so much pain"
My guide answered, "Yes, but from it strength you did gain."
I asked, "Why was I alone and where was everyone then?"
He said, "Someone was always there so look again."

It was then the truth became clear
My guide was God and He'd always been near.
During the hard times, He heard my heart's cries
Reaching out His hand to me, He helped me to rise.

He believed in me
Knowing all ready the person I would go on to be.
The broken pieces of my heart He healed
Beauty inside me He revealed.

"It was You who gave me the strength to go on"
"In your life I was never gone."
Tears started up again as I saw everything was going to be okay
For when I felt weak, God carried me, helping me hold on for one more day.

Living For More

Time stands still for no one
The past cannot be changed for its over and done.
With days passing by so fast, we can't live looking back in regret
But where we came from, we'll never forget.

Hard times each of us has faced
Situations have even left us feeling misplaced.
We've been hurt by the ones we held dear
On our own we challenged our darkest fear.

Along the way we lost some we love
They're never gone though for now they watch from up above.
Things we said to others that we didn't mean
Our true friends always stayed so that on them we could lean.

There were those in our lives who walked out
Thinking it was our fault, we struggled with self-doubt.
When they left, our hearts bled from being broken apart
Not knowing what to say we wondered without them where to start.

Some of us grew up in homes filled with violence
Afraid to speak out, we lived a life trapped in silence.
The abuse caused us to grow up way too fast
Years later, we still bare the scars left behind from the past.

We found ourselves walking on life's ledge
As we barely hung onto the edge.
At times everything just seemed so far away
Lost and alone, we drifted from day to day.

No, it was never our fault these things happened
But, my friend, this is not the end.
I know you hurt and still feel pain
One result from the past was that strength you did gain.

Who you were back then doesn't define you today
For allowing yourself to heal, you've grown in many a way.
Over certain circumstances you had no control
Yet it doesn't mean that you're still in the victim role.

To those who've been hurt in love, you'll find it again
Give yourself time though and don't worry about when.
The right one will continue to wait
When that day comes, how beautiful the love

will be that you create.

For those who have lost a loved one, they're never gone
In your heart their memory forever lives on.
Know that they walk beside you
Watching over you, they are around in spirit to help you get through.

For those who have had friends walk out, let them go
They're not real if they leave when about the hard times they know.
A true friend loves and accepts you for who you are
They choose to stay, letting you know they're never too far.

For those who have been abused, take all the time you need to heal
A survivor myself, I understand the nightmares and pain are real.
It's ok that your feelings and emotions you release
Let your heart mend piece by piece.

We can't go back and rewrite our past
There's a future to write about that is endless and vast.
Yeah, mistakes we'll make
What's important though is from them the lessons we take.

Only one life we get to live

But we have a chance to turn it into something beautiful and positive.
Once a moment is gone, we can't get it back
So every opportunity presenting itself we need to grab hold and track.

Fear should not keep us from living the life we want
We're stronger and tougher than the demons that taunt.
The key is not thinking about what could have been
Picture what can be and discover the courage within.

There are countless possibilities that can be ours if we only accept
Pursuing our dreams is the concept.
This life is worth fighting for
We must take the chance to live for more.

Before It's Too Late

In an empty bedroom, a young woman looks around
This used to be a happy place where laughter and joy would abound.
For this room once belonged to her best friend
Taking everything in, she still can't believe what happened.

The room is exactly how it appeared before
Only her beautiful friend isn't here anymore.
It seemed like just yesterday the two were laughing and carrying on
Then, in one unexpected moment, she was gone.

Walking over to the dresser, she picks up the diary left behind
Somehow she knows that if she reads it, her friend won't mind.
The familiar, girlish handwriting brings tears to her eyes
As she reads the first entry, she's overcome with grief by the memories.

Everyone always said the two were inseparable

Outgoing and cheerful, being the life of the party they were quite capable.
All through childhood they stuck together like glue
Everything about each other they knew.

Back then they were so young and innocent
Having such a wonderful friendship was the best present.
Nothing could break the bond they shared
Alone in life they never fared.

Even in high school between them things didn't really change
Although after graduation, different paths for themselves they had to arrange.
Their goals led them other ways to get their own start
But keeping n touch, they never were that far apart.

While she stayed single, her friend got married to a wonderful guy
What she didn't know was the marriage was based on a lie.
A few times on the phone, she detected something in her voice
Yet each time her friend assured her she was happy with her choice.

From so far away she couldn't see all the violence
She never suspected her friend lived a life trapped in silence.

A happily ever after all the photos revealed
No signs showed the bruises concealed.

Sometimes when she visited, the husband acted cold
Always a different explanation for his behavior she was told.
"It's okay, he's just going through a hard time," her friend would say
Yet in her mind she sensed something else was going one each day.

Finally one day her friend confided in her
Giving her all the details about the abuse that would occur.
With tears in her eyes, she said she feared going back
That she couldn't continue fighting off each attack.

The two friends made plans for her to leave
But no further word did she receive.
Then one day on the news she saw the report
For beating his wife to death, the husband was in court.

Into a million pieces broke her heart
Anger raged inside her that he tore her life mercilessly apart.
If only she had known sooner about the hell he put her through
Maybe she could have saved her friend by telling her what to do.

Now she stands in front of her friend's tombstone
Without her, she feels so alone.
A life cut short by abuse, she didn't deserve to die
The question screaming inside is Why.

Placing a rose on the grave, she pays her final respects
Many other lives the death of this beautiful woman affects.
Silently she says a heartfelt prayer for all victims trapped in a cruel fate
She prays help will come to them before its too late.

Inside This Heart

Looking at me, it's only what I show on the
outside that you see
Too focused on the scars I bear, you really
don't know the real me.
I all ready know you're forming assumptions
about what I didn't say
But I'm confident in who I am so it's okay.

In order to really know me, you have to see my
other side
The one that out of sight I usually hide.
There's more to me than just what lies on the
surface
If you don't look beyond, though, my story
you'll miss.

A fragile and broken soul to some I may
appear
Let me tell you, I've learned how to conquer
my fear.
Others can try to run away from their history
No shame do I have in mine because it helped
make me.

The truth about my experiences I won't deny
Forsaking my heritage would be living a lie.

Family history in my life doesn't need to repeat
For I broke the cycle rather than wait for a cruel fate to meet.

Yet my life I never take for granted
It's seeds of hope that in this world need to be planted.
Not everyone makes it out alive
I'm fortunate to be here today after managing to survive.

Still people like to tell me that I can't make it on my own
I guess they don't know that for others' actions I had to atone.
My whole life I've always found a way to pull through
Even when I had no guidance and direction showing me what to do.

I even hear how I'm too young to know what I want
But I'm older than you think due to battling demons that haunt.
Age has nothing to do with choices I make
I all ready have what I want because I'm happy to give and not take.

Every time I pass up the easy way out
Following my heart, where I'm going I carry no doubt.
When it comes to the truth, I will always stand strong
Once in this life I was lost, but now I know

where I belong.

Go ahead and form your own opinions about me
But for who I am from my lips you won't hear an apology.
The title of survivor I bear with honor and pride
Forever by my fellow survivors I'll fight side by side.

The faith I have in myself cannot be shattered
Because I'm no longer that victim once battered.
I picture what can be instead of what could have been
Then I discover the strength and courage within.

It isn't a prize that I fight for
My goal is to help others find their open door.
The greatest reward comes with making a difference
Knowing that in someone's life I can be a positive presence.

It doesn't matter if others doubt my ability
That I continue to believe in myself is the key.
Nobody can tear my life apart
For I'm the only one who knows what lies inside this heart.

Imagine

As survivors, we've seen and felt so much pain
Beneath society's labels, though, we bear more strain.
Covering up the truth, they treat us as if we have a disease
With their myths and taboos, they don't help put our lives at ease.

The stereotypes that go around only create more hate
Because ignorance leads the way, innocent lives are left to suffer a cruel fate.
Cries for help remain silenced and unheard
That anything bad like abuse could happen they find absurd.

What they don't know is what they fear
So it's easier for them to pretend they can't hear.
For those of us who have survived, we lead the life of an outcast
This long we were never expected to last.

When speaking out, we are the ones judged and accused
But it was never our fault that we were abused.

Our stories they regard as merely a lie
Over and over again, the truth they attempt to deny.

This isn't how we should have to live
Always fighting off all the negative.
In this world, we deserve to have a voice
No one has the right to take away that choice.

How different would it be if our real selves we didn't have to hide
If people took the time to see the beauty inside.
What if our true feelings and emotions we could release
Without the fear of others tearing us down piece by piece.

People would finally hear us out
Speaking freely, we could show them what we're really about.
The stigmas associated with us would be erased
By the real truth they'd be replaced.

Removing our masks, we could expose who we are
Accepted instead of scorned, they wouldn't ban us to somewhere afar.
What happens in the life of a victim and survivor they'd learn
No longer afraid of the unknown, life for the better would take a new turn.

If people left their hearts open, down would

tumble the ignorance barricade
Then in life, it wouldn't feel as if we were beginning to fade.
Trying to see from our perspective, they'd start to understand
Suddenly, working together, more would lend a helping hand.

Pain and suffering could be relieved
With open arms, victims and survivors would be received.
Strengthening in numbers, we could win this fight
As we watched justice make things right.

Those still trapped in darkness would be rescued
Going to a safe place far from the brutal feud.
They wouldn't live on a bloody, violent battlefield
A better life free from abuse we could help them build.

It will take work to make this change
But it's not impossible if things in our own lives we arrange.
First the difference we want to make in this world we imagine
Then taking action, we follow through and carry out what we envision.

Why Not Me

She walks alone in the rain
Her heart heavy with so much pain.
The rain hides the tears on her face
But no one's around to see them in this deserted place.

Just as the sky is dark and gray, so is her past
It's for this reason she's wandering the streets as an outcast.
People don't really know what she's been through
They only analyze her and pretend they do.

Rejection and betrayal seem to follow wherever she goes
Friends hear her story and suddenly turn into foes.
Outside the circle she gets tossed
With nowhere to go, she feels completely lost.

Shivering against the cold, she pushes on
Everything in her life appears to be gone.
Through her tears she can hardly see up ahead
Emotionally drained, on the inside she's almost dead.

This isn't how she planned her life to be
One that's left her isolated and empty.
A never-ending battle, negativity she must fight
Unlike the fairytales, she has no rescuing knight.

On her own she stood her ground
Even when flaws in her others found.
Amidst the ignorance she used her voice
Yet they tried to silence her by taking away that choice.

They dismissed the truth as nothing but lies
The louder she spoke out, the more they began to despise.
Still, she refused to keep silent
Exposing the truth about how life can be cruel and violent.

The rain now pours down in a blinding torrent
Soaked to the bone, she wonders why on this mission she was sent.
It's not fair that she is falsely accused and put on trial
While the entire time she's forced to fake a smile.

She feels she's walking the green mile for a crime she didn't commit
With their hate, they push her closer to the edge of the pit.
Stereotypes are tough to break through
Especially when the truth is covered up by

those who knew.

Looking around, others are content and at peace
But could they be hiding emotions they haven't been able to release.
For there's a story waiting to be told in everyone's heart
Just as there are voices wanting to be heard before they fall apart.

Suddenly she knows that she needs to keep speaking out
For ignorance can't be destroyed if they don't know what the truth is about.
It's more than worth the fight
Making a difference is about helping others see the light.

The sun starts to shine and she doesn't sink below
To a hurting world in need, compassion she'll show.
In the sky a beautiful rainbow she can see
Now instead of thinking "why me" she thinks "why not me."

A Survivor Is.....

A fearless warrior on life's battlefield

A compassionate soul reaching out to others

A voice speaking out for those who have gone unheard

A beacon of light for those trapped in darkness as they guide them to safety

A guardian angel protecting the innocent from harm

A comforter whose insight gives them empathy for fellow victims and survivors

A leader stepping up to pave the way for future generations to come

A ray of hope through the tough times

An encourager who provides inspiration with their story of survival

A phoenix that is rising above the ashes of the

past

A fighter who seeks justice

A hero who sacrifices to help save lives from being shattered apart
A defender of the truth who stands up for what is right

A beautiful person whose inner beauty shines bright

An eagle that is soaring to new heights

A source of motivation for those rebuilding a new life outside of abuse

A courageous person making breakthroughs in life

A strong soul who has overcome the odds stacked against them

A confident soldier in this fight who never backs down or gives in

A dreamer who believes in themselves and their work they are doing

An explorer who sees beyond the horizons to find the destiny waiting for them

An extraordinary person accomplishing and achieving great things in life

A caring person who shows the world what love and compassion are all about

An empowering person who envisions what can be instead of thinking what could have been

A heart of gold helping others to heal in their own journey

A voice loud and clear that refuses to be silenced

A blossoming flower who continues to grow in strength, beauty, and wisdom

An insightful person who shares their knowledge to tear down the walls of ignorance

A listener who hears the cries of other hearts out there

A gentle soul not afraid to show emotions and feelings

A team player that unites together with other survivors to fight for the freedom of others

A positive person making the difference in someone else's life

A healer putting back together the broken pieces of another's heart

A butterfly flying high and taking off towards a new day

An author writing the pages of a better sequel to their life's story

An adventurer who takes risks and chances, seizing opportunities that come their way

A tough sailor who endures the storms and still stands strong after the rain is gone

A teacher that educates the world on the dangers and damages of abuse

An artist painting in bright positive colors for those facing negative shades of gray

A Good Samaritan loving with all they have to love and giving with all they have to give

A hardworking soul making the most of each moment in life

A carefree spirit enjoying the present, looking towards the future, and leaving behind the past

A priceless, precious gift filled with so much worth and value

A lending hand to those in need

My Voice, My Choice

For a long time I lived in silence
Questioning if I should talk about the violence.
I even wondered if what I went through was real
That it was all in my head and I was delusional is how you made me feel.

I did my best to pretend nothing happened
But the memories of those days don't just end.
You say to let it go because it took place years ago
It doesn't matter how much time passed because the scars still show.

There was a point where I tried to run away from my history
I found out that I can't escape something that is part of me.
The events of my life make up who I am inside
Good or bad, my story I don't want to hide.

So many years of my life were robbed since I didn't speak out
You made sure I covered for you by creating in me self-doubt.
All those lost years I'll never be able to regain

They were ones filled with so much pain.

When I walked away, I left the past behind
Emerging a stronger person, no trace of who I
once was will you find.
Life has given me a second chance
Taking back control of my life, I'm no longer
under your trance.

It's been quite a journey to get this far
I had to work hard to repair a self-image that
you managed to mar.
Rebuilding my life has meant putting back
together the pieces of my heart
As I recover the dreams and goals you tore
apart.

In your eyes, no real value did I hold
Lucky for me, I don't always listen to what I'm
told.
I know you never had high hopes for me
All on my own I discovered what I could be.

I've risen from the ashes and taken flight
My past allows me to reach out because it gave
me the gift of insight.
This knowledge I have I want to share
Then maybe more people will start to care.

I might be just one person but I believe I can
make a difference
Walls of ignorance need to be destroyed for
they block the truth's presence.
Even if it means putting myself out there, I'm

willing to make that sacrifice
Standing steadfast, I won't give into
temptations that entice.

What I see are lost souls searching for
something more
They need guidance in learning how to soar.
Their hearts' cries I can hear
I'll be that someone that fights with them as
they face their fear.

This world is in need of faith and hope
With a bit of encouragement, people won't let
go of their rope.
The power of love goes a long way
It helps others to survive another day.

Looking around, I glimpse the hurt behind
each face
They wonder if they belong in this place.
Someone to save them is what they long for
Because on them people have slammed the
door.

I've stood at that point of no return
Feeling the secrets of the past inside me burn.
The greatest strength I found within when I
thought I couldn't go on
I had to remind myself that those days were
gone.

What you put me through I turned into
something positive
You actually fueled the fire that helped me

fight to live.
I refused to let you hurt me and get the best of me
For your actions I all ready paid but no more will I pay the fee.

Now loud and clear I speak
Knowing the past made me strong, not weak.
Why I share my story everyone may not understand
To a world hurting, I'll lend a helping hand.

So many trapped souls still wait to be rescued
Innocent lives are caught in a violent feud.
Whatever it takes to get them out and expose the truth, I shall use my voice
This is my passion, my calling, and my choice.

Together We Can

Life isn't always positive and bright
For us survivors, we've had to put up one big fight.
Sure, we're still here standing strong
But that doesn't mean we don't have those days where we feel we don't belong.

Smile is what we always hear
So that all is okay with us we make it appear.
No one sees through the mask we hide behind
They have no idea that ourselves we're trying to find.

It's not easy to be our real selves when people don't understand
Society labels us instead of lending a hand.
From stereotypes to myths, we endure the hate
Because on society's social scale we fail to rate.

Scars are the only thing they notice
The truth they ignore so us they dismiss.
People fear what they don't know
Viewing us as different, the ignorance starts to show.

Inner beauty isn't what they look for

If they did, then they'd realize that to us there is something more.
Instead they focus only on the outward appearance
Since they can't relate to us, they never grant us acceptance.
Our stories often go unheard
Not believing us, they think we're absurd.
In their ways they're set as certain guidelines they go by
Yet if we prove them wrong, everything they'll deny.

Why can't we live side by side and co exist
Rather than being categorized on some list.
We aren't treating them like they're an outcast
So why do they continue to judge us based on the past.

Making life out to be glamorous and perfect is not reality
The cold, hard truth people need to see.
Battles and struggles we face are very real
There will be tough times while we allow ourselves to heal.

These things we shouldn't have to sugarcoat
Because that's living on a false note.
When people only hear the good side, the overall perspective they don't get
False illusions blind them to the challenges we've met.

As survivors, we need to let the truth be

known
What really takes place in the lives of victims and survivors should be shown.
How will people learn about what goes on
If we keep pretending that the pain is completely gone.
It's okay to have bad days and still grieve
When we release the tears, more healing we receive.
We don't have to put on a charade that nothing's wrong
Expressing our feelings and emotions is what makes us strong.

Even when people leave, we survivors still have each other
Fighting side by side, we're there for one another.
We no longer have to face the world on our own
Together we can make a difference and a change, knowing we are never alone.

Measure of a Heart

Isn't it amazing how someone can enter our life and take us by surprise
Taking us by the hand, the good things about ourselves they help us realize.
The footprints they leave on our hearts last forever
Teaching us how to fly again, they aid us in each endeavor.

That special someone in my life is you
Staying by my side, the hard times you've helped me get through.
I never expected our paths to cross at a time I felt pain
But now I know the meaning of what's one man's loss is another one's gain.

When others saw flaws, you saw the real me
Someone else you didn't expect me to be.
It's as if you looked straight into my heart
Picking up the pieces, you began to heal every broken part.

Most of my life I wandered around lost and confused
Insecure because people abandoned me after I

got used.
Walls I built up so I wouldn't get hurt anymore
Yet you tore them down, showing me I was worth fighting for.

You opened my eyes to see life does have moments that are beautiful and positive
Just as I started feeling numb inside, you gave me a reason to live.
I'd almost given up, thinking there was nothing more my life held
Then you came along to tell me it was never my fault and I hadn't failed.

Hearing my story, you didn't run away
Instead you made the decision to stay.
My emotions and feelings you let me freely express
Knowing the truth, of me you never thought any less.

I don't know what I did to deserve someone like you
Because in this world friends like you are rare and few.
Meaning into my life you brought back
As you help me rebuild it and get on track.

For the first time I feel more alive
Having you here makes it easier to survive.
My dreams and goals you encourage me to follow
Shining your light, into a stronger person I'm starting to grow.

After the storm you are my rainbow who brings me hope
Restoring my faith, I have something to hold onto as I climb back up my rope.
Because of you I'm learning to open my heart again and take a chance
Believing that onto a better life I can advance.

I've begun to view myself in a new light
You repaired my damaged wings to prepare me for flight.
Now I see far beyond the horizon
Up ahead, with you in my life, waits a future brighter than the sun.

This friendship though doesn't only go one way
I'll always be here for you every day.
You can count on me to be there to break your fall
I believe together we will make it as we keep standing tall.

No matter what comes our way, in us I believe
You've made a difference in my life and I know anything you can achieve.
Flaws I don't see for all I see is someone who's given me a new start
You are amazing to me because of the measure of your heart.

Only So Much

I should have walked away a long time ago
If only I knew then what I now know.
But it's better now than never
Too bad the family couldn't stay together
forever.

At one time a close-knit family we appeared to
be
Back then, though, so many things I failed to
see.
Little did I realize this was one big charade
Eventually true colors showed as the rest
began to fade.

A family feud tore everyone apart
All of us were left with a broken heart.
Now divided, we went different ways
The distance continued to grow through the
days.

I'm not even sure what sparked this flame
But no one owned up to being wrong as
elsewhere they placed blame.
Trying to keep peace, in the middle I got
caught
As I watched you destroy one another the

more you fought.

For a while, I just let things slide
I didn't want to take either side.
Only one part of the story would I ever hear
Yet family business was told to more than one outside peer.

To me the truth no one wanted to tell
For other people, though, the whole story you did unveil.
Why was I left out in the dark when they knew
With them it had absolutely nothing to do.

Still, I kept up a good appearance
Going along with the normal family look
under a false pretense.
I thought that I could get everyone together
but I was wrong
Learning the hard way, I saw how you made me feel I didn't belong.

My own family turned their backs on me
That I wanted to live my life you couldn't see.
For you so many sacrifices I willingly made
In the end, it didn't matter because I was betrayed.

Too busy holding grudges, you treated me like an outcast
All because you refused to let go of the past.
You never really heard anything I had to say
It was easier to ban me when I didn't follow your way.

Oblivious I never was to anything that went on
I just wish that sooner I would have been gone.
Nothing will ever change because you have too much pride
Since you refused to make amends and instead lied.

I've gotten this far on my own
Even when you knew about the hard times, you left me alone.
By pride this family was destroyed
Now as I live my life for me this drama I choose to avoid.

In order to move on I have to say goodbye
I can't keep walking on eggshells and living a lie.
Unlike you, who I am I won't fake
It's my turn now as I cut ties because only so much can I take.

Trading Places

I had my life all planned out how I wanted it to be
Where it would eventually take me I couldn't see.
My life didn't turn out exactly like I thought
Some of the most valuable lessons from my experiences I was taught.

Most of the dreams I had were shattered
For the longest time I played the victim battered.
Home certainly wasn't a heart-warming place
I received pain instead of a loving embrace.

Often I wondered why all this pain I felt
Why was it that a cruel hand in life I was dealt.
I imagined what a perfect life would be like
In my own life it seemed I had received my third strike.

Traveling alone, no one understood where I had been
Because of their ignorance, it was hard for me to let anyone in.
Mentally comparing myself, I didn't feel good enough

People always told me to just suck it up and be tough.

The more I fought on my own, the more lost I became
Not everyone liked that the title survivor I chose to claim.
Remaining strong for myself, I didn't have much guidance
The only things I had to follow were my heart and conscience.

Many times the question why stayed on my mind
Seeing others living happy lives, I felt left behind.
For so long the truth about who I was I decided to hide
It left me feeling like a stranger who looked in from the outside.

I found myself thinking why can't I be normal like the rest
Instead here I was battling memories causing me to be depressed.
Then I realized normal doesn't exist
I am who I am and people shouldn't categorize me on some list.

At one time I wished I could go back and change my life
The truth is I grew stronger because of all the strife.
I do not regret what I've gone through with

each trial
It's during the hard times I find strength to go another mile.

True, I grew up around violence in a broken home
But I discovered who I was when away from it I began to roam.
I wasn't running from the problems that came my way
Rather I faced those challenges to move onto another day.

You won't see me stoop down to my abusers' level
To do that would allow them in my life to still rule.
I've learned from every mistake
Keeping it real, my life I refuse to fake.

It may take me awhile to heal
At least, though, my emotions I'm not afraid to feel.
What matters is not where I came from but where I now stand
Even when I fall, on my feet I always manage to land.

Yes, a part of me is a little girl on the inside
That little girl I carry and protect during life's tough ride.
From the life I had before I bear no shame
Being a survivor is something I'll proudly claim.

As I continue to heal and grow, new things I find out about myself
A risk taker at heart, I won't let my life waste away on a shelf.
In second chances I strongly believe
What doesn't kill me makes me stronger is what my mind has started to conceive.

No, my life didn't turn out exactly according to plan
However, in my vocab, "I can't" is replaced by "I can."
When it comes to my dreams, I don't know any limit
To me, I'm not really living if on the sidelines I sit.

Would I go back and change my past
No because then I wouldn't be this warrior on life's battlefield who's continued to last.
Despite all the pain, I haven't allowed myself to fade
For this reason I say that places in life I would never trade.

Know Who You Are

This world can be such a cold place to live
Sometimes it seems the negative outweighs the positive.
Pressure is put on us to be a certain way
If we don't measure up to society's expectations, we pay.

Acceptance isn't something easy to come by
Especially when we're expected to live a lie.
Flaws and imperfections they wait to point out
Never good enough in us they create self-doubt.

We're pulled in different directions as this way and that we go
Society's rules people continue to blindly follow.
A distorted image of themselves in the mirror they view
They wouldn't see that if how beautiful they are they knew.

Yet many self esteems are torn apart
Because overlooked is the beauty of one's heart.

True identities are left unrevealed due to fear
Traumatic events that people have endured no one wants to hear.

In their own comfort zones they stay
Having nothing to do with anyone who has the courage to find their own way.
They think we are rebels and outcasts for being different
But into the darkness of ignorance we refuse to be sent.

To the world's ways we don't conform
We choose to keep our hearts open and warm.
Their views are not always right
Just to be heard we have to fight.

Most of the time alone we stand
Since it's hard to find someone to lend us a hand.
Towards us people can act so fake
In their minds, they're keeping count of our every mistake.

It isn't for them that we are living
Making the most of our lives, our best we are giving.
They haven't traveled the path our shoes have walked on
Not understanding what we suffered, they are quick to be gone.

The real battle comes when on the truth we shed light

There are those who don't want to see us take flight.
They attempt to keep us trapped in silence
Hoping word doesn't get out about abuse and violence.

Yet after years of being quiet, we owe it to ourselves to speak out
The only way myths are dispelled is if we tell what our stories are about.
Who we are we should not sacrifice
"To thine own self be true" is great advice.

Each of us has real beauty that shines through
It can be seen in how we act and the things we do.
That's something we should never change or trade in
Even if others find us negative, somewhere every story has to begin.

Within every heart lies a story waiting to be told
People need hope on which they can hold.
When it comes to important matters silence is not golden
Society needs to know we aren't the same people we were back then.

For too long the truth has been concealed
It's time that the other part of our lives be revealed.
Who cares what others think or say when we take this chance

By speaking out, we have an opportunity in our lives to advance.

The world cannot steal way our honor and pride
Stepping up, we won't sit on the side.
With us change has to start
In making a difference in this world we can play a part.

Let's not allow them to destroy the values we hold dear
We've become warriors who have conquered our fear.
No matter what they say we'll continue to go far
Standing up for what we believe, we know who we are.

You Are Beautiful Because....

You are beautiful because you take the time to be there for others.

You are beautiful because you are not afraid to express your emotions and feelings.

You are beautiful because you lend a helping hand to those in need.

You are beautiful because after all you've been through, you're still standing strong in life.

You are beautiful because you open your heart to others and show compassion.

You are beautiful because you accept people for who they are, without judging them.

You are beautiful because even when things look negative, you always see the positive.

You are beautiful because you encourage those who are hurting as you inspire them with your words.

You are beautiful because you really listen to what others have to say instead of dismissing them.

You are beautiful because while others only see scars and flaws in people, you look beyond and see the beauty of one's heart.

You are beautiful because you shine your light into the dark places of people's lives.

You are beautiful because you never stop believing in yourself and in others.

You are beautiful because you fight to make a difference and a change in this world.

You are beautiful because you allow your voice to be heard, refusing to let others silence you.

You are beautiful because you have risen above the ashes of your past and have transformed into an eagle ready to take flight.

You are beautiful because you picture what can be in life instead of thinking about what could have been.

You are beautiful because on the battlefield of life, you don't leave anyone behind.

You are beautiful because you heal people's hearts with your love.

You are beautiful because you sacrifice to save those who are lost and trapped still.

You are beautiful because you hear and answer the silent cries that come from people's hearts.

You are beautiful because you survive the storms of life and always find that rainbow in the sky after the rain.

You are beautiful because even when times are rough, you never give up but keep on pushing on, knowing that you will make it.

You are beautiful because you take people by the hand and you walk beside them down life's road, never leaving them to travel alone.

You are beautiful because as you continue to heal and grow, you also help others to heal and grow in their own journeys in life.

You are beautiful because you motivate others as you help them to see the good in themselves.

You are beautiful because you are a voice for those who have not been heard.

You are beautiful because you take chances and risks in life, always finding that open door and seeing beyond the horizons.

You are beautiful because you help others

achieve their own dreams and goals, helping them to realize the potential they have to keep going far.

You are beautiful because you give with all you have to give and love with all you have to love.

You are beautiful because you never compromise what you believe in or what you stand for even if it means you have to stand alone.

You are beautiful because you show the world how beautiful life can really be.

You are beautiful because you protect the innocent and speak out about the truth.

You are beautiful because you choose to embrace the future with wide open arms as you rebuild your life and make the most of it.

You are beautiful because you share your story and experiences to spread awareness and reach out to fellow victims and survivors.

You are beautiful because when society puts pressure on people to act and be a certain way, you remain true to yourself and follow your heart, daring to be who you are.

You are beautiful because you step up and pave the way for future generations to follow as you leave your own footprints in this world.

You are beautiful because you do all you can to break through the ignorance that keeps people blinded and expose the truth about what really goes on.
You are beautiful because you are willing to go above and beyond and go that extra mile to make someone smile or to cheer them up.

You are beautiful because you show that you truly care about what others go through.

You are beautiful because you don't know any limits when it comes to achieving your dreams and goals in life.

You are beautiful because when others tell you that you can't do something, you look them straight in the eye and tell them that you most certainly can as you continue to climb those mountains in life.

You are beautiful because you have such grace, humility, and dignity about you and you never take your life for granted.

You are beautiful because while others are boasting about what they have done to get into the spotlight, you work quietly behind the scenes because you are more concerned about helping people in life.

You are beautiful because you don't dwell on

the past but write new chapters for your life's sequel to reach that happily ever after and see how it all turns out.

You are beautiful because you believe in new beginnings and seize those opportunities that come your way.

You are beautiful because you let those you care about know how much you love them and appreciate them every single day.

You are beautiful because your heart overflows with generosity and kindness for others.

You are beautiful because you are a courageous warrior fighting for your right to live an abuse free life, using the strength you have within to face the challenges and fears that try to stand in the way.

You are beautiful because you take time to enjoy the simple pleasures that life holds.

You are beautiful for all these reasons and more, but most of all you are beautiful simply because you are you.

Out On The Battlefield

The hardest part is over or at least that's what they say
Little do they know about the challenges we face each day.
We may not be victims anymore
Yet still we're haunted by the memories of before.

They expect us to forget and move on
Don't they realize that part of our life will never completely be gone.
What happened to us we can't simply erase
For those were dark days filled with pain we had to face.

It was never our fault so we shouldn't feel shame
Unfortunately, we've been the ones forced to carry the blame.
Even people on the outside point the finger without knowing the real story
They only see what they want to see.

Despite what others think, being a survivor is no easy task
Often we hide our fragile side behind a mask.

Insecurities from our past still whisper in our ear
Bringing back to mind all our old fear.

Not only were our hearts broken but our self-esteem was shattered
No words can really describe accurately the abuse we suffered.
We each have different stories and none of us has been through it all
However, those traumatic events we can vividly recall.

Unless they've been in our shoes, they don't know about the life we lived in silence
How our innocence was taken from us amidst the violence.
No matter what type of abuse we endured, it left many an after effect
Instead of listening, our stories into pieces they begin to dissect.

To live as if nothing ever happened is what they expect
Acting like we're being negative if on our past we reflect.
As a survivor, life isn't always going to be positive
We have those days that the memories we relive.

Why should we live a lie to cover up the crime
Isn't it enough that the torture we endured lasted such a long time?

In a moment our lives were changed and nothing was ever the same
We waited for someone to come save us but no one ever came.

The pain left us feeling forgotten, forsaken, and desolate
With no one to hear our heart's cries, we watched our lives start to plummet.
Even our families turned their backs on us as our trust they betrayed
Over and over again, we're the ones who paid.

Now here we are continuing to fight to survive
Holding onto hope, to get a new beginning we strive.
Healing from scars and wounds completely won't happen right away
So we must take it one step at a time, day by day.

We're not alone though for others out there can relate
They, too, were forced to suffer a similar fate.
We survivors need to join together and unite
Speaking out, on the truth it's time to shed light.

All the trials in our lives we've risen above
Showing just how strong we are when push comes to shove.
Knowing what it's like to go through it alone, innocent lives we can protect and shield
Making sure it doesn't happen to them as we

fight for them out on the battlefield.

Before You Say Another Word

Who are you to tell me who I should be
When it's only my scars and imperfections you see.
Only pieces of the story you choose to hear
Perhaps it's because what you don't know you fear.

Why don't you get the facts straight
Instead you twist words around with your hate.
Go ahead, blame me and act like it's all my fault
At least I'm not the one attacking you with a verbal assault.

The things I went through you'll never really know about
Yet you sit there pretending you have it all figured out.
Funny but I don't recall you ever being there in that time and place
So there's no way you can begin to tell me about what I had to face.

Even before I speak, you've made up your mind

Always some flaw in me you have to find.
You only see the side of me that I show
There's still so much about me that you don't know.

With me you are constantly trying to compete
Living my own life, your challenge I refuse to meet.
Are you that desperate for attention that you have to boast
Expecting everyone to give you a congratulatory toast.

It isn't about who does more
What matters is helping others find their open door.
To you this may be a competition
But being myself, I'm not looking for an award to win.

All the answers you think you hold
Your own values for acceptance you sold.
I don't have to pretend to be someone I'm not
To expose the truth and keep it real I've fought.

By putting me down what are you hoping to gain
Seems to me you're acting like the one who caused you pain.
I have no problem admitting I'm not perfect
Your opinions of my life, though, won't have any effect.

In my shoes you've never walked a mile

Therefore, you haven't endured the exact same trial.
Within your own little comfort zone you hide
Ignorance blinds you so you can't see what's on the outside.

Remove the blinders and you'll see reality
Trust me, some things in life cause people to pay a costly fee.
Mistakes each of us are going to make
What matters are the lessons from them we take.

Judging others may be what you do best
Remember, though, one day you'll be put to the test.
They say that what goes around comes around
When that time comes, there may not be anyone to help you off the ground.

Are you truly happy with who you are
Because loving and accepting myself has helped me get far.
So go ahead and say what you want about my life being cursed
Before you say another word, take a look at your own life first.

Every Step of the Way

It's been about seven years since you last hurt me
I was just a teen when I made the decision to break free.
Out on my own, it was better to be a stranger without a name
Than to be a part of a family where I took all the blame.

I knew you'd never admit to what you did because it isn't your style
Everything I learned has been through many a trial.
When confronted, the truth you denied
Suddenly I became the one who about all this lied.

At least, though, I can say I tried
No longer do I have to hide.
If I waited for you to own up to your actions, I couldn't move on
Forgiving you, I cut ties, accepting from my life you were gone.

In me you refused to believe
Thinking that nothing great in my life I'd ever

achieve.
Hanging on for a while, I thought you might come around
Instead you attempted to knock me to the ground.

Pointing the finger at me, I was falsely accused
Yet it was you, not me, who abused.
You never wanted to change
Using control, my life you tried to arrange.

You just couldn't look past the scars you created
Every little imperfection and flaw about me you hated.
You didn't think I would ever amount to much
Telling me you saw me as nothing more than a failure and such.

That's when I knew I couldn't continue to stay
Knowing the time had come for me to walk away.
In going my own way, you probably thought me weak
But I found the greatest strength when I found my voice to speak.

I knew it wouldn't be easy to face this life alone
Yet for your actions I no longer wished to atone.
You were right in saying I'm stubborn and strong willed
My determination has made me quite the warrior on the battlefield.

What you put me through helped prepare me all along
Now I work hard to right your wrong.
I'm thankful I didn't take after you
That I would make it in life I guess I somehow always knew.

Many challenges I've had to meet
Motivation to rise above is that past history I won't repeat.
Time has shown me who I am and what I can be
New things in myself I'm beginning to see.

Every dream is worth fighting for
How much courage I have I discover when thinking I can't take much more.
When I think I won't make it, I remember what I survived in the past
It reminds me that through anything I can last.

Your approval isn't needed for the life I now live
To get the life I wanted I first had to endure the negative.
I'll never forget where I came from or how I started out
With every step of the way, I begin to see what my true calling is all about.

Survivor Guidelines For Rising Above in Life

Accept others for who they are

Believe in yourself and the work you are doing

Challenge ignorance with the truth

Determine the right path to take in life

Embrace the opportunities that come your way

Fight for your dreams and goals

Give with all you have to give

Help those in need every chance you get

Imagine the kind of life you want to live

Jump in, making the most of each moment

Knock out negative thoughts and feelings by having a positive attitude and outlook in life

Love the person that you are

Motivate those around you to keep holding on

Never compromise the values that you hold so dear

Open your heart and mind to new ideas and possibilities

Press onward towards your destination that awaits you

Quench drama by ridding yourself of negative influences and cutting ties to those that try to bring you down

Reach for every dream as you climb new heights

Stand strong for what you believe in

Take pleasure in the simple things in life

Use what you've learned from the past to better your future

Venture out and explore what lies beyond the horizon

Walk away from those who hurt you and seek to destroy you

Xrcise your rights to live an abuse free life

Yield not to the demands and expectations of your enemies

Zero in on your goals as you achieve them and turn them into a reality

Never The Same

At a crossroads in her life she's approached
To survive the trials along the way herself she coached.
Everything about her past she has tried to bury
Still, so much pain from the memories she continues to carry.

No one knows all the dark secrets she hides
Facing it alone, there's not one person in whom she confides.
Her whole life she's been a weary traveler going from place to place
Worn out and exhausted, she wonders if she can endure this race.

Finding somewhere she belongs has proven difficult
Rumors about her spread since her they won't first consult.
They haven't walked this road so they don't understand
Maybe if they were there, they would see how it was and give her a hand.

The bruises on the outside have long since gone
Yet the scars on the inside linger on.
Physical pain came and went for it didn't last
But staying forever with her is the emotional pain from the past.

It all began when she was just a young girl
Growing up in a broken home, the violent events started to unfurl.
The abuse was never her fault for she was young and innocent
Many nights, though, she wondered why to this hell she'd been sent.

While other kids were happy, she fought to live
Doing the best she could to remain positive.
Their expectations she didn't measure up to or meet
Then the cycle once again started to repeat.

From verbal to physical abuse the attacks grew vicious
She never knew when it'd happen after something went amiss.
Behind closed doors, she released the tears
Locking herself in, just beyond the door lurked her biggest fears.

Eventually she learned to disappear
Always sensing when those violent, dangerous outbursts were near.
Blending in with the background, she let herself fade
More than anything this life she wanted to trade.

She never imagined home would be a prison cell

Trapped in silence, there wasn't anyone she could tell.
Ignoring her, she felt the emotional abandonment and neglect
In their eyes, their daughter was a worthless reject.

They tried to cover it up as they put on a false pretense
Disregarding the issues at hand, they cared only about their public appearance.
Throughout her childhood, love she didn't receive
The only thing keeping her holding on was in an escape she continued to believe.

Surviving the childhood trauma, she made it out alive
For a better life she chose to strive.
Step by step, her life she began to rebuild
Knowing the past chapters were all ready sealed.

Even now, she struggles with wounds left behind
The missing pieces of her heart she's still trying to find.
People tell her to just let it go
That you never forget these things they don't know.

Looking back, she wishes sometimes it would have been different
Instead of leading a life where into exile she

was sent.
Of her own life she now has control
Yet that of an outcast she still plays the role.

She's just now getting her self esteem back
As she attempts to heal from damage and get her life on track.
There are moments she thinks what it would have been like to have love
Then maybe she'd been treasured and cherished like she was an angel from above.

The past, however, cannot be undone
To have a better life, though, she can't be scared and from it run.
Every challenge she must stay and fight
Otherwise her goals and dreams will vanish out of sight.

Taking a step forward, she chooses the path pointing to her future
More than anything, that this is her time she's sure.
Without looking back, on a new part of her journey she decides to embark
Allowing the light in, gone is the dark.

Out there, anything is possible
Believing in herself, she sees how life can be beautiful.
Those simple pleasures make it worth holding on
A brand new day in her life is beginning to dawn.

It's her heart she follows
Knowing that faith and hope are with her
where ever she goes.
She can't change the past, but she's free from
guilt and shame
From this day forth, living for herself, nothing
will ever be the same.

One Of These Days

I never knew what I could really be
Until the day I finally broke free.
For so long I couldn't see the real beauty
locked away
All I heard were the negative things you had to
say.

The whole time I possessed this strength inside
Discovering the true potential I held I didn't
have to hide.
You wanted to keep me trapped underneath
your control
Yet deep within me laid a warrior's soul.

Your expectations for me I shattered
This survivor's heart was not completely
battered.
I guess you didn't think I could be so tough
That all changed when I showed you I had
enough.

Maybe you thought I was beyond hope
But I pulled myself up and climbed back up
my rope.
Unfortunately for you, into pieces I didn't
break
In fact the strong person I am you helped
make.

You underestimated me by thinking me weak

My real power came when finding my voice I began to speak.
After that the darkness started to fade
Without you around into my life its way the light made.

How clearly everything appeared
When I learned to face that which I feared.
Something good came from all this pain
A new perspective on life I was able to gain.

It is true that from bad situations good can arise
Experiences I endured taught me lessons, making me wise.
My eyes were opened to the many possibilities
Those chances waiting for me I began to seize.

Out of the ashes my life I rebuilt piece by piece
No longer was it up for lease.
I watched as the pieces fit back together again
Victory in overcoming my past I knew I could win.

My own dreams I set out to cultivate
It's amazing how from the wreckage a beautiful life I did create.
With a little bit of hard work, I pulled through
The key was believing in myself and what I wanted to do.

Through every storm my faith and hope have helped me to survive
Taking nothing for granted, I am truly thankful

to be alive.
You assumed that out on my own I'd fall flat on my face
Picking myself up, I look to the future as every promise it holds I embrace.

To live my dreams your approval is not required
Of this healing journey I haven't tired.
When I look back on the past, I think of the odds I beat
How on each occasion I rose above the challenges I had to meet.

A fragile, handle with care sign I don't wear
Because the broken parts I've had time to repair.
I will always stand for the truth
Maybe one of these days you'll quit seeing me as the scared girl from my youth.

With a Little Bit of Hope

Shattered hearts lie in pieces on the floor
Screaming inside, people say they can't take much more.
With the walls closing in, they start to suffocate
Their only thought is will someone help before it's too late.

Vacant eyes stare straight ahead
So many words they want to say are left unsaid.
All the pressure and demands of every day life are taking their toll
Now, falling into a pit of despair, depression gains control.

For so long, they've had to face everything on their own
Misunderstood and unheard, they carry on alone.
Their lives are like unopened books sitting upon a shelf gathering dust
Secrets from their past to no one will they entrust.

Those hidden chapters no one has gained access to read
With pain from the nightmares the words on the pages bleed.
It's a part of life they'd rather not talk about
Still haunting them, those memories they wish they could do without.

Such horrible stories many would find hard to believe
Unless you'd been there, the thoughts are not easy for your mind to conceive.
Trapped in darkness, they saw how hell did exist
Enduring torture and abuse, they were silenced if they tried to resist.

Unloved and unwanted, they were recycled along
Put on them was the blame for all that went wrong.
Having no home to go to, they travel an empty road now hollowed
As they watch the remains of their dreams begin to erode.

Lost, through the days they continue to drift
Trying to find the missing pieces, among the wreckage they sift.
Where to start they aren't even sure
Out here for a broken heart they search for a cure.

The fears and insecurities of the past they want to leave behind
Because who they really are they long to find.
Time is something they can't turn back
If they could then they'd prevent each attack.

So far away they wonder if anyone can hear their cries

Coming to the surface, the real pain is hard to disguise.
A safe place they wish to run away to
Somewhere that in the midst of this chaos someone would come to the rescue.

Yet with no guidance and direction, they don't know which path to take
The only thing they know is heartache.
Invisible, they stand on the edge of the crowd unnoticed
What they feel is never mentioned or discussed.

As we pass by strangers on the street may we reach out a hand
Beneath that smile beats a heart that yearns for someone to understand.
An encouraging word freely give
People need to know there are those still positive.

Let us be the ones to show them compassion and love
Bestowing kindness, we can let them see the beautiful moments life is made of.
They need something to hold onto that helps them get through the day
With a little bit of hope, in themselves they'll believe, knowing it will be okay.

My Prayer For You

I found myself thinking about you tonight
How on your own for a while now you've put up a brave fight.
You've been through so much more than people realize
If they took the time to really know you, they'd be in for a beautiful surprise.

I've watched you weather some rough storms that came your way
Standing strong, though, you persevered to see another day.
Even when you felt you had lost everything, you hung on tight
The promise of a brighter future you kept in your sight.

No complaints did you make when by others you were betrayed
Motivated even more, you showed them you wouldn't fade.
Giving it all you had you proved you weren't going anywhere
Believing in your dreams, your faith from you they couldn't tear.

Through the rain you continued to smile
Never backing down, you stood for truth when the rest lived in denial.
Fame and popularity meant nothing to you
Your mission was to simply help others get

through.

A more selfless person than you I've never met
Nothing in return do you expect to get.
To give people a better life so much you sacrifice
The world would be a positive place if others were that nice.

True to yourself you always remain
Reaching for the stars, your goals you attain.
In your eyes I see the spark of hope
The answer you refuse to take is nope.

Humility I notice about you as you keep it real
Your true feelings you're not afraid to feel.
Times you fell you got right back on your feet
No obstacle in life can have you beat.

People have told you that you wouldn't get far
Your self-perspective they've tried to mar.
Yet to possibilities you kept an open mind
Leaving all the senseless, useless drama behind.

I know you still have battles you face
It's not easy sometimes to run this race.
So here's my prayer for you
Those hard times may these words carry you through.

I hope you know by yourself you don't always have to be strong
If you feel out of place, I'll show you where

you belong.
What's on your mind please don't be afraid to speak
No matter what you've gone through, I'll never think of you as weak.

The fragile parts of your heart you don't need to hide
You have no reason to be ashamed of your other side.
Without it you would not be who you are
Beauty is to be found beneath every scar.

You'll never fight out there on your own
Because I won't let you go through things alone.
Here with me you'll forever have a home
I'll be the light you see when in the dark you roam.

Don't allow anyone to steal your pride
They can say what they want, but I'm on your side.
Who you are you don't have to compromise
I hope you know how much you mean to me when you look into my eyes.

Most of all, I pray that your true worth you see
Inside your heart is courage and inner beauty.
One of a kind, you cannot be replaced
By your friendship my life has been graced.

Oh, and one last thing before I go
You, my friend, are my hero.

I love you for who you are and what you help me to be
You're the missing piece in my life that holds the key.

Remembering the Silent Victims

All too soon you've flown to somewhere far away
In a better place you are where everything is now okay.
No one ever really knew your name
To the world, just another statistic your death became.

Yet they never saw what behind closed doors went on
Now your voice has been silenced forever since you're gone.
There was no one around to witness your pain
Scars and bruises you covered so they wouldn't look at you in disdain.

Home turned into the one place you didn't want to go back to
Trapped, with nowhere to go, you weren't sure what to do.
In the dark you sat alone as tears streamed down your face
Beatings you received instead of a warm, loving embrace.

Your self-esteem they ruthlessly destroyed
Having no love shown to you, in your life you felt a void.
Every night you lay awake
Afraid that for their anger a target you'd make.

Bruises and black eyes became more common
Each time you thought to yourself, "not again."
On this battlefield, the war grew more intense
Trying to protect yourself, you fought back in self-defense.

How could love turn to such rage
Where daily in a fight for your life you were forced to engage.
This shouldn't have happened to an innocent soul
You didn't deserve to be cast into that role.

Yet your heart's cries went unheard
Living in a hellish nightmare, they never had a chance to be answered.
On your behalf not one person was there to intervene
The only ones who knew were the ones who found you at the crime scene.

By then it was too late
Tragically, your life had been cut short in the hands of a cruel fate.
If only help would have come sooner, you might still be alive
Even till the end, you fought bravely as you tried to survive.

The world never had an opportunity to know who you really are
Those who hurt you took away your right to go far.

Instead of protecting you, your last breath they watched you breathe
That someone could crush a human life like that is hard to believe.

Sadly, many cases of abuse don't get heard
Some question the truth, thinking it absurd.
Not all victims live to see another day
Too soon they become angels who from this cold world fly away.

How many more lives will be sacrificed because no one will hear
These innocent souls shouldn't have to live in fear.
What will it take for the truth to finally be seen
In some households, abuse is part of the daily routine.

It is in memory of the silent victims we survivors fight
Remembering them, their untold stories we recite.
We'll do whatever it takes to save those still residing in silence
No more lives should be lost because of violence.

Better Than That

You pretend everything is all right
Yet on your skin are bruises from another fight.
The tears you hold back
Still, each night, you fear an upcoming attack.

His vicious words cut you to the core
Becoming a stranger, he's not the same guy you knew before.
Kisses and hugs by scars are replaced
All signs of affection have been erased.

In the comfort of your own home, for your life you have to fight
Hiding among the shadows, you try to stay out of his sight.
Every time he goes out you feel a little bit relieved
Then too soon he returns and quickly shows he's peeved.

Once again you become his scapegoat
With you the guilt and shame you're forced to tote.
When he leaves again, you break down
Wondering why he removes your smile with a frown.

You find yourself in a deadly game of cat and mouse
Your opponent is none other than your spouse.

He says he loves you but you know his words are lies
Looking at him, you can see the truth hidden in his eyes.

Hanging around, that things will change you want to believe
Putting it all back together is what you hope to achieve.
Deep down inside, though, you know it will never be the same
The longer you stay, the more pain you'll endure as you take the blame.

Trust me when I say that I've been there before
Straight down the middle my self-esteem tore.
Walking on eggshells, the next attack I never knew when to expect
He'd interrogate me and point out every defect.

Nothing got better but only worse as time went on
Finally I felt that I, too, was almost completely gone.
Attempting to pick myself up, under his abuse again I shattered
Thus the cycle repeated as I continued to get battered.

Until I made the decision to leave, my wounds could not heal
Because each time I took him back, new pain I would feel.

Saving my own life, I broke free
The promise I made to myself was never again would I pay that fee.

Do not put yourself in danger for fear of being alone
Help is out there so you don't have to face it on your own.
Abuse is not love
For real love doesn't hit, hurt, or shove.

Never sacrifice your life for someone who doesn't care about you
Hell and nightmares are not worth going through.
Live a life where you're shown respect
Not one in which you always hear that you are imperfect.

If he can't love you the way he should, walk away
Your life you'll risk by continuing to stay.
Think about your safety for it comes first
Don't stick around to see things reach their worst.

You are someone very beautiful
Who should know what it is like to feel special.
You truly are worth so much more
Break free, refusing to return to that life of before.

The choice may not come easy to make
Freedom can only be obtained when that first

step you take.
You shouldn't have to be trapped in silence, surrounded by sorrow
For you deserve better than living in fear, not knowing if you'll see tomorrow.

Painted On Smiles

Everyday you pass strangers on the street
Smiling at you, they never let on about challenges they daily meet.
All around you are stories that have gone untold
As people try to find something in life on which they can grab hold.

The faces you see mask the emotions they really feel
In their minds, they're questioning what's real.
Each day to them seems the same
Walking alone through life, they are the ones without a name.

No one's ever taken the time to listen and hear them out
Instead the validity of their stories people doubt.
Getting preached at, they're told to heal quietly within
Because to talk openly about a painful past is considered an ungodly sin.

So rather than be judged, they remain silent
Knowing the finger will get pointed at them, they dare not even vent.
For them it's easier to blend into the background
Then by those who despise them they won't be found.

The more they keep quiet, the emptier they feel inside
The truth about what they endured they shouldn't have to hide.
Yet from those who haven't been there they are ripped apart
Till they begin wondering if anything is left to their heart.

Others say not to look back on the past at all
Out of sight and mind, though, it doesn't just fall.
The memories of those times they can't simply forget
Those were some terrifying moments that they met.

Ignorant remarks make them feel uncomfortable and out of place
Society casts them aside, refusing to welcome them in an open embrace.
In muted misery they continue on
A major piece of their life now gone.

At night they lie awake, tears soaking the pillow
From the heart wrenching sobs every emotion starts to flow.
Written on the pages of a journal are the words they can't say
That was a different era in which they lived a different way.

Sadly, by the past they are defined

When others only see the scars that were assigned.
It doesn't matter that their lives are now on track
People choose to look behind, bringing up things they've tried to leave back.

No one tells them it was never their fault
They only add to the pain their own verbal assault.
Aren't they the ones lecturing to let it go
Why then is it someone else's life they are obsessed to follow?

Life is hard compared to what they ask
Obviously they haven't lived the tough life that survivors mask.
In their perfect little fantasy worlds they dwell
How the rest should live they proceed to tell.

Wake up and take a look at those around
Reality is most come from a rough background.
You're not helping them heal by telling them to keep quiet
Whether you know it or not, inside they are battling an emotional riot.

Get off your high horse and step into real life
Where daily people fight to overcome strife.
Because they wear a smile, you don't suspect what's really wrong
You're too busy issuing orders to say where they belong.

Do you even know how many lives are falling apart
Since no one will aid in mending a broken heart?
Don't be fooled by the painted on smiles
Start reaching out to help the hurting make it through those trials.

Stronger Than You Know

After all I've gone through, you'd think I'd give up by now
Yet through the tough times I continue to plough.
I've always believed that greater things I could achieve
It all depended on how my life I chose to perceive.

This road in life has not been an easy walk in the park
With faith and determination on a new journey I embark.
From an early age I learned how to fight
Amidst the trials, somewhere in my heart a fire started to ignite.

People didn't think that a girl like me would ever succeed
They were too busy looking at the life I used to lead.
Betting against me, they expected me to fail
But I wasn't born a quitter who on hard times would bail.

The free ride in life I refuse to take
Because a stronger person detours and shortcuts I won't make.
Hard work has gotten me this far
There's more to me that lies beneath each battle scar.

I watch as others give up and on the sidelines reside
Who I am though I know I don't have to hide.
Experiences I went through helped me grow
After the storms in life, I always found my rainbow.

No, it isn't going to be sunny, blue skies all the time
However, I'll never know what's on the other side until those mountains I climb.
To throw dreams and goals away would be a waste
Why turn back now after everything I've faced?

True I have had my share of sorrow
But it has been my strong will that's given me hope to hold onto tomorrow.
It does no good for me in self-pity to wallow
I strive to rise above, not sink below.

Outlook determines where I'll end up
In this life there's no room for drama and gossip.
I can give people something to talk about
When they see me making it instead of dropping out.

To give up or keep going is ultimately my choice
On behalf of the silent victims and survivors I choose to be a voice.
My past is over so I look to the future to

discover what it will hold
Beyond the horizon opportunities and
possibilities unfold.

In another direction I'm being led
For the first time I feel so alive as this new path
I tread.
Nothing is impossible when my heart I follow
I'll keep surviving because I'm stronger than
you know.

Enough Said

There was a time where I trusted you
Knowing you'd be there no matter what I went through.
Then right before my eyes you changed into a different person
Your heart became one made of tin.

How it happened I don't know
But a new side of you began to show.
Pointing the finger at me, accusations you threw my way
All because I decided choosing myself first was okay.

Your only line of defense was I have a bad attitude
Yet I'm not the one being rude.
We may be from the same family
You have yet to see the things I've had to see.

Sure we grew up in the same household
Always for acceptance your soul you sold.
The abuse you never had to suffer
So you have no idea how bad things really were.

You've never felt the pain I've carried
In fact, from you I kept secrets buried.
Everything about me you don't know
Criticism upon me you freely bestow.

Tell me, have you had your heart broken apart

Surviving an abusive marriage, are you struggling to get a new start?
So many people you've dated in your past
Using them, you haven't known what it's like to find a relationship that will last.

For a long time I faced challenges alone
Taking the free ride in life, you can't stand on your own.
Opportunities you waste and throw away
I fight for what I want every single day.

My way in life I right fully earned
While mistakes you repeat because you still haven't learned.
Sacrifices for you I made
Betraying me, this is how I'm repaid.

I've worked to get this far
Along the way I received many a scar.
At least I'm on the right track
Building my life piece by piece, I am taking it back.

You walk around as if you're so superior
Yet having very little to show for your life, you don't make me feel inferior.
I look at you and see someone just like Dad
Abusive traits you possess that he had.

Family history I refuse to repeat
I won't give into defeat.
On my own dreams I'll achieve
It doesn't matter that in me you don't believe.

This time your decisions by yourself you'll have to make
Your hateful attitude I am not going to take.
Keep on talking all that talk
At least I can talk while I walk.

My life to yours I used to compare
Going down another road, more about me I care.
My thoughts and beliefs I won't compromise
Because I couldn't live covered in lies.

Call me a hypocrite
I didn't let the fire go out that in me was lit.
When it comes down to it, I'm the one working to get ahead
Looking at where we both are, I think enough has been said.

Putting Aside Differences

In a society where ignorance prevails, it can be hard to take a stand
It's easy to lose your way when no one reaches out a hand.
People don't always look at the picture overall
So they fail to see the heavy burdens others haul.

Too many times who they really are they compromise
Anyone that comes along who dares to be different they despise.
Their morals and values fall out of place
Judgmental, they slow those down trying to run life's race.

The problem is they never stand on the outside looking in
If they took a step back then maybe they'd see the story within.
Yet they continue to walk on
While all around are hurting hearts with pieces gone.

Silently struggling, true feelings people hide
No one ever knows that they're battling another side.
Too often opinions are formed about the past
Because people haven't been there, peers they are quick to blast.

They think everyone else from their mistakes

should learn
When it came to living their dreams, they missed their turn.
Now how the rest should live they proceed to tell
Like a puffed up peacock their pride begins to swell.

That one needs to have a degree is what they say
We're more than qualified since we experienced the trauma every day.
There's street smart and book smart
Combined together, both work to teach one how to get a new start.

Some things, though, in a classroom can never be taught
They are best shown through personal battles fought.
One has no right to assume they know all about someone else's life
For each of us have endured different levels of strife.

No situation is ever exactly the same
From various backgrounds we all came.
If we're survivors, why are we fighting against each other
Uniting together, we should be helping one another.

None of us have the answers to every single solution

Sharing our ideas, together we have a chance to actually win.
Stop the preaching for it won't do any good
For the battlefield save the fierce attitude.

It's time we start showing each other respect
Otherwise our words and actions will not have much effect.
Why sink to the level of those who broke our heart
We're no better than them when we tear others apart.

In order to make a change we must set a good example
Once we step up we're regarded as a role model.
But if we war with fellow survivors who will take us seriously
Immature behavior on our part is all they'll see.

We don't want to be like the rest
It's bad enough that this world violence and hate have begun to infest.
Abuse is what we're here to prevent
That's why we were sent.

Let's work together as a team
From our own eyes let's remove the beam.
Putting aside differences, for peace we need to strive
As we create a world that's a bit more positive and alive

Freedom In Tears

I've always been the type to hide a part of myself
Afraid if I opened up, my heart would be placed on the shelf.
I was never great at saying how I truly felt
It was easier for me to be quiet about the things I'd been dealt.

A life of pain I didn't plan for
So many experiences left my heart broken and sore.
Not asking to go through it, circumstances were beyond my control
Without my consent I got cast into the victim role.

What I learned back then I'll never forget
But I proved to myself that I could overcome obstacles met.
That my past was preparing me I didn't suspect
Miracles happen, though, when them you least expect.

Still, for awhile barriers and walls I put around my heart
Distancing myself, alone from the rest I stood apart.
In places I stumbled and fell
Yet I refused to let the tears begin to well.

For answers I searched within my mind
The reason I suffered I wanted to find.
Everywhere pieces of me were scattered
Losing grip, to the floor my thoughts shattered.

Of nothing could I make sense
Insecurities plaguing me, constantly I was on the defense.
Somehow in the storm I got lost
Finding that survival at times came at a cost.

Living in my own world I felt isolated
To the point everything about myself I hated.
Inside my heart broke from being used
The scars served as painful reminders of when I was abused.

I didn't want people to think me transparent
Keeping emotions locked away, I wouldn't vent.
I figured it was easier to throw away the key
Then the other side of me no one could ever see.

My past I didn't know how to explain
Without having people think I was insane.
Publicly and openly feelings I couldn't show
Some things people don't need to know.

I wanted to cry but the tears were gone
Bleeding inside, I wondered if I could carry on.
A part of me had died
I needed to protect this exposed fragile side.

Then one day I realized no longer could I hold back
After trying so hard to be perfect I needed to give myself slack.
For what happened I'm not the one to carry the blame
In the history that makes up me there is no shame.

Now I eliminate the unnecessary guilt
Knowing there's a new life for me waiting to be built.
I don't have to be strong on my own
Because in this life with friends that care I'm never alone.

I'm learning to let loose a little more
Times aren't like they were before.
I'll continue to challenge and fight all my fears
Allowing my emotional dam to break open, I find freedom in tears.

It Starts With Me

Everyday is not always positive
To move on to a better life has become my motive.
People say life is only about dancing in the rain
They forget that we can't just block out the pain.

My life is not an open book for all to read
Yet on my personal feelings and emotions people feed.
There are plenty of things I've left unsaid
Somehow, though, to false assumptions my words led.

I've seen my share of sorrow
But if I only focused on the bad, I wouldn't see tomorrow.
Each moment may not be perfect
However, I never view being a survivor as a defect.

It's not all about rainbows and butterflies
Moving on means cutting the negative ties.
Still over the past I allow myself to grieve
Knowing through my tears, locked up feelings I relieve.

For learning purposes it's okay to look back on the past
It helps us to grow more even though it didn't

last.
If we never made mistakes, then what would we learn
Hard times teach us valuable lessons so to those ways we don't return.

Stepping back, the future I want I envision
For it's ultimately up to me whether I lose or win.
My time can't be wasted on caring what others say
Yesterday has passed and now it's a new day.

In some areas I'm fragile but I won't break
Who I am today, battles I've fought have helped to make.
The strength of a survivor don't underestimate
For overcoming challenges, we beat fate.

If storms never came, my rainbow I couldn't find
How far I've made it the past serves to remind.
To the level of those who hurt me I refuse to stoop
I know I'm better than that and won't get caught in that loop.

No longer am I a player in their cruel game
Standing for truth, I share not one part of the blame.
The person I am is not necessarily influenced by my background
I changed and began to heal so the girl within could be found.

Breaking the cycle, a prisoner I didn't want to remain
By sitting on the sidelines nothing could I gain.
I took a chance at opening my heart
With some soul searching, I discovered how to get a new start.

Only one life do I have to live
So my all I'm going to give.
Past events can't be erased
But wisdom and insight emerged from what I faced.

At the bottom of the ladder I may stand
Perseverance leads me to climb up it hand over hand.
Character and personality contribute to true beauty
Keeping it real, with me what you get is what you see.

Others can drop out of life's race
I'll never lose my sense of dignity and grace.
Let them take their lives for granted
No matter where I end up, I shall bloom where planted.

The story of my life I'm only just starting to write
Nothing's going to put out my light.
Hope for a better way of life I see
To make it happen it has to start with me.

Unbreakable

With no regrets I look back on my past
Thankful that those days didn't last.
About the events of my life people want to speculate
But I know in my heart I was fortunate to escape a cruel fate.

What I endured I wouldn't wish upon anyone
I only wish that from that life sooner I would have run.
Back then, though, no one helped me to leave
Daily emotional and physical pain I did receive.

Even now those feelings words can't accurately describe
To keep me from speaking out they tried to offer a bribe.
Yet a deadly weapon is silence
Because it covers up the unknown violence.

The term survivor makes people think I'm weak
Only bits and pieces of my story they hear when I speak.
It took strength to decide to walk away
Not looking back, I left without having a word to say.

For the first time I wasn't surrounded by fear
The negative things people said about me I chose not to hear.
In order to make it, in myself I had to believe
I couldn't worry about the way in which me people would perceive.

I know I'm not the same person I used to be
It's not my problem if only the scars others see.
Through the storms I've managed to survive
Even on my own I continue to stay alive.

I wouldn't go back and change anything about my life
What's made me a stronger person is fighting through the strife.
Always the under dog, no one expected me to ever win
But a warrior at heart, I found reasons to live again.

Once on the verge of defeat, I held onto all I had
Keeping my eyes on the light, I focused on good instead of bad.
There are struggles that I still face
However, it's okay I'm not perfect and who I am I embrace.

Beyond the surface is more than meets the eye
It took strength not to give up when I wanted to die.
At times I stumbled and faltered

Picking myself up again, the hard times I weathered.

I wouldn't be who I am today if not for lessons learned
Now I'm in control of my life since the tables turned.
Maybe I don't know exactly where this road will lead
But giving it my best shot, I believe I'll succeed.

In my faith I am firmly grounded
Knowing to be here still standing I've been blessed.
Giving in just isn't my style
Speaking out loud, I have come out of exile.

There's no handle with care label on me
I haven't broken during this journey.
Under pressure I won't shatter
Despite past events, I smile and share in laughter.

The heart inside of me beats for something more
Onto my dreams and beyond I soar.
Every piece of me is still intact
Not breaking then and not breaking now, I won't be cracked.

This Moment

Sometimes life comes at us so fast
All too soon the years go by and we reminiscence about the past.
Looking back, we see how events shaped us to become who we are
From yesterday to today we've made it pretty far.

There were times we thought we wouldn't survive
Always though it was our faith and hope that kept us alive.
In the middle of the storm we found ourselves caught
Weathering the rocky times, with us perseverance we brought.

The role of the underdog we took on
People expected that by now from life we'd be gone.
When we thought we wouldn't make it we pulled through
Discovering within us a strength we never knew.

Damaged goods is the label for us they used
They didn't realize how strong we survivors are who have been abused.

Anything but fragile we've risen above
For we won't be the ones stuck when push comes to shove.

On our own we had to learn to fare
What others thought of us we didn't care.
Either stay trapped or live in freedom we had to choose
Having the hearts of fighters, our lives we weren't ready to lose.

No white flag of surrender would we raise
Never did we imagine how our stories of survival could inspire and amaze.
In the battle for our life, we were determined to still be standing
With faith we believed we'd find a safe landing.

Though our wings tore a bit, they began to mend
The days of an abusive past finally came to an end.
Now the healing process could begin
As control over our own lives we started to win.

Today we bear no guilt or shame
Working together, we let others know they aren't to blame.
Transforming, we don't resemble the victims of before
Still hanging on, we know our lives hold so much more.

We're thankful to still be alive
Our battle is fought in memory of those who didn't survive.
While people take their lives for granted, we know it hasn't been easy
Yet even amidst the ugly areas, we see the hidden beauty.

Many miles we traveled to get this far
Despite hard times our fighting spirit no one can mar.
Dwelling not in the past, we make the most of the present
For rebuilding ourselves and living to the fullest starts with this moment.

Someone Somewhere

Ignorance is a disease that tears the world apart
Keeping people in the dark, society doesn't want them to get smart.
Many important issues go unaddressed
To the truth about these things on one ever confessed.

Those who want the attention make helping others all a show
Taking the credit for everything, their name they desire people to know.
Yet who they truly are they don't always appear to be
Taken by their charm, that they have no place to lead others fail to see.

Attacking those who have nothing to do with them, they create drama
In reality they are no better than the ones that caused them trauma.
But basking in the glory, they soak up the spotlight
Blocking the people that are sincere in the fight.

When petty battles over popularity arise, the real battles can't be fought

Too busy outdoing each other, in their own game these "leaders" are caught.
Me, me, me is the attitude they perceive
Lies and broken promises they get followers to believe.

Real heroes, though, do exist
Ones who aren't concerned about making any A-list.
Silently they work behind the scene
What they say they actually mean.

Picking up the slack, broken pieces they begin to mend
Messages of hope and faith throughout the world they send.
They don't fight for glory or fame
Instead they help because they once were victims carrying shame.

Remembering what they suffered, the nightmares for others they wish to prevent
Because to live that life no one is meant.
Day and night the pain these angels on the battlefield relieve
Giving people a reason to once again believe.

No words do they even have to speak
Quietly listening, they show survivors they're anything but weak.
In times of trouble they don't look away
The truth they aren't afraid to come out and say.

Though unseen, the effects of their work clearly stand out
Believing in their mission, about what they've done they don't shout.
Self-sacrifices and compassion heal many a broken heart
Positive role models, they teach others how to get a new start.

Not all leaders are superficial and fake
There are those more concerned about giving and glory they won't take.
Next time you feel alone and wonder if there's anyone who does care
Remember even if you can't see them, out there working to make a difference is someone somewhere.

Make It Back Through Anything

Along a twisting, winding road you travel
What you've seen and felt makes you wonder how life can be so cruel.
None of it you ever asked for
In silence the hidden pain you bore.

Things didn't turn out exactly as you planned
Many times you got knocked down when you tried to stand.
Your side of the story people never gave you a chance to explain
Instead they left you alone to walk in the rain.

You watched as pieces of your life fell apart
Bravely, though, you smiled while suffering a broken heart.
From the past you weren't sure how you'd recover
Walking a fine line, you just wanted it all to be over.

The haunting memories with you stayed
For others' mistakes you paid.
Their frustration and anger they took out on you
Damage caused you couldn't go back and undo.

Trying to forget, you ran away
In combat you found yourself with the demons of yesterday.
Everywhere you went they followed
With them new insecurities they towed.

No one was there to tell you it wasn't your fault
So shame and guilt you carried from the assault.
All you needed was to just be heard
For someone to believe you and not disregard your word.

I won't pretend to know exactly what you went through
But I am here to stand right beside you.
You are not responsible for what happened
It isn't your fault so your life story please don't end.

I know the nightmares were very real
Sometimes the wounds take a long time to heal.
Yet even with your back against the ropes, you put up a fight
Forever searching and reaching for the light.

This road you don't have to travel alone
You shouldn't have to face this on your own.
A true survivor you are at heart
Just know it's okay if you need to cry and fall apart.

You've been through so much all ready
Shining through is your inner beauty.
Never give up on this life
Remember you've proven you can make it
back through anything despite strife.

Face In The Crowd

Out on the streets she searches for a place to sleep tonight
The events at home she tries to put out of mind and sight.
At such a young age gone is her innocence
Memories lingering on she can still feel her abuser's presence.

At least out her no one knows her name
They don't even suspect that from a broken, violent home she came.
Blending in, she gets by unnoticed
She doubts that back at home she's missed.

It all happened so fast
Torn apart by violence her happy family didn't last.
Somehow she became the scapegoat
Drowning under the pain, her life resembled a shipwrecked boat.

The visions of every fight replay in her mind
Now she travels alone to leave it all behind.
With no direction or guidance, she isn't sure where to go
But to return to that place would cause her to sink below.

Bruises and scars she's managed to conceal
The emotional pain in her heart feels very real.
Lost and alone, she continues to push on
Wondering where her life has gone.
Her heart has begun to rip at each seam
Leaving without a word, she knows there won't be any search and rescue team.
The remaining pieces of her youth she holds in her hand
How love can turn to hate she doesn't understand.

Staying to herself, beneath a cloak of invisibility she's able to hide
Betrayal taught her to be careful and in others not quickly confide.
Strangers surround her but never glance her way
Even if they spoke to her, she'd have nothing to say.

Every mile takes her farther from home
To places unknown she starts to roam.
This isn't really the life she expected
Better to run away then stay where she was unprotected.

For her a life of freedom was worth more than a lifetime of pain
Taking the risk, a new beginning and identity she wishes to gain.
Who she is she wants to discover
Making her stronger are the trials she has to endure.

It's worth it when her sense of purpose she can achieve
Climbing that ladder, in her dreams she'll believe.
Tonight the answer she searches for whispers clear and loud
Angels in disguise walk with her so she's not an unknown face in the crowd.

If I Knew Then

The question what could have been plays on my mind
As right in front of me the past begins to rewind.
One important reason, though, it serves
To show me how strong I was to get around life's curves.

Some people look back and things they regret
For me, it's a learning experience I'll never forget.
Hard knocks taught me how to really survive
Making me more thankful to still be alive.

Strangers tell me they're sorry for what I went through
Saying that won't take away things I can't undo.
I want them to be glad for me that I'm here
To view me as a fighter who fought through my fear.

Those storms couldn't keep me flat on my back
With renewed courage I countered each attack.
Events happened beyond my control
But it remained up to me if I played the victim or survivor role.

Life doesn't always go according to plan
You learn to improvise and do the best you can.
The whole picture you have to be able to see
Then you'll find beneath the dark areas the hidden beauty.

It's not about asking if you could go back and make changes would you
The real question is to make your life better, what are you willing to do.
Right here, right now is the moment you should be living for
Instead of looking behind you, look at what lies beyond the open door.

We've all had our share of heartache
Where we felt the pain would cause us to break.
That edge we slowly approached
To back away from it ourselves we coached.

Our past to our future was a steppingstone
The more we heal, back together the pieces of our hearts are sewn.
Stronger we become when we get through every trial
Regarding who we are we don't live in denial.

With these changes going on, nothing ever stays the same
We're different today than we were in the days from whence we came.
It's up to us how this life we view

If we keep an open mind we can start anew.

I don't think about how differently things
could have turned out
That this is where I'm supposed to be I have no
doubt.
Would I change things if I knew how it would
be back then
No because I don't ask why, I ask when.

The Other Side of Life

Life can be truly amazing and beautiful
Sometimes we forget that when we only focus on parts that are cruel.
Although we've been through hard times, we're still here
By taking on those challenges, we battled our every fear.

The storms have given way to sunshine
No matter what crosses our path, we know we'll be fine.
If we really look for it we can see the color among the gray
It's the smallest things that let us know it will all be okay.

Pleasant surprises find us when we least expect
With them they carry a more positive effect.
They show us that life does have a beautiful side
Taking a chance, sometimes we need to sit back and enjoy the ride.

Focusing on the pain too much makes us see more negative
It's okay to let loose and allow ourselves to actually live.
Over us the past no longer has complete

control
The moment we broke the chains, we freed our heart and soul.

Now beyond the horizons we can take flight
Opportunities we missed before wait in plain sight.
A new world we've entered
One in which we are not a caged bird.

Yes we went through hurtful experiences but a better life we deserve
Not one where from danger we continuously have to swerve.
We lived through hell and yet we managed to survive
So proving to ourselves we can be the odds, for victory we should strive.

Too many times darkness creeps in, blinding us to the light
Doubt causes us to question if we're really right.
Standing for what we believe, those feelings cast far away
Because if we weren't strong we wouldn't have made it to see another day.

Our lives took a turn but it doesn't have to be for worse
In us lies the power to break the past's curse.
Love and trust may not be easy to come by
But we'll never know them if we don't open our hearts and try.

It's okay to feel a little bit afraid
The special moments that make up your life don't ever trade.
True, venturing into the unknown may be scary
However depending on how you view it, it can hold untold beauty.

If we only open our eyes new things we discover
For when it comes to writing our life story we are the author.
Changes it's time for us to create
Because the other side of life does patiently await.

Steps To Allowing Yourself To Heal

Always believe in yourself

Break ties with those who only bring you down and have a negative outlook in life

Challenge and confront your problems, taking them on one by one

Discover the inner strength and power you possess by digging deep into your soul

Embrace the beautiful person that you are

Find an outlet or hobby that lets you freely express yourself in your own way

Grieve over the past and allow yourself to cry

Hear what people have to say and really listen without passing judgment

Impact and impress those around you by sharing your story and being yourself

Join with others to make a difference and change in this world

Know what you want in life and go after it

Lead by example and be a positive role model for other survivors and victims

Meet your own expectations for your life and don't worry about others' expectations for you

Never compromise your values and morals

Open your heart to trust and love again

Pursue your goals as you advance onto better things

Question the ignorance of the world and shed light on the truth

Release the locked up emotions that you've kept inside

Speak up and out for those who have no voice

Turn your dreams into reality

Use your past as a way to better your future

View yourself as a strong survivor as you remind yourself of everything you've overcome to get this far

Write out your thoughts and feelings

Xrcise your right to live an abuse free life as you rebuild it from the ashes of the past

Y is not the question to ask; instead ask yourself why not you?

Zoom down life's highway but not so fast that you miss out on the simple pleasures in life that create those big moments that make life enjoyable

A Strong Survivor....

Isn't afraid to show emotions

Reaches out a helping hand to those in need

Owns up to their mistakes while taking responsibility for their actions

Gives credit where it's due instead of taking all the glory for oneself

Turns something negative into something positive

Not too proud to ask for help from others when needed

Sees the hidden beauty buried beneath the gray areas in life

Looks beyond the outer surface of a person and sees to the heart

Listens to what others have to say without making judging remarks or false assumptions

Steps back and tries to see things from another person's perspective in order to understand them better

Respects another person's opinion without tearing them down

Gives back rather than taking

Doesn't make a show out of helping others

Fights for those who aren't able to fight for themselves

Serves as a voice for those who cannot speak out

Shows compassion towards fellow victims and survivors without being harsh and critical of their stories

Keeps going even when feeling like giving up

Defends and stands up for the truth against society's lies

Never backs down or compromises morals and beliefs

Dares to be oneself rather than being like everyone else

Stands grounded and firm in what they believe

Gives hope to others by sharing their own story and speaking out

Searches beyond the horizons in life to find something more to live for

Knows and believes in their mission and calling in life, refusing to walk away from it

Uses the things of the past as a way to motivate and inspire fellow victims and survivors

Discerns when to say goodbye and cut ties by not allowing another to verbally or physically abuse them any longer

Surrounds themselves with positive people who will help build them up as they restore their lives and make something new of it

Never says statements such as "I know your pain"; "I've had it worse than you"; "I've gone through the same thing as you" and other ignorant remarks like that because they know that everyone is different and that no one's situation is ever exactly the same

Learns to love oneself again and accept all of oneself

Remains humble, not taking any part of life for granted

Expresses gratitude to those who have been there for them

Lets the important people in their life know

how much they care, appreciate and love them every single day

Takes chances that will allow them to better themselves and get further in life

Chases after every dream, turning it into a reality

Doesn't stereotype or judge others

Teaches and leads others by stepping up but also learns from others as well

Saves others out there trapped in silence but also allows others to save them

Has no shame in who they are or where they come from for it has been replaced with pride of knowing they've survived and beat the odds in life

Shows the world what they are made of when the world says they can't do something or won't make it

Never makes excuses for why they can't do something but finds reasons for why they can

Asks what they can do to make their life better rather than asking what they could go back and change in their lives if they could revisit the past

Proves to oneself what they can rise above instead of trying to always prove themselves to others

Doesn't make life a competition but focuses on living their own life and making improvements necessary to help them grow more as a person

Enjoys those simple pleasures in life that add up to the big moments that can't be put into words

Lives up to own expectations they have for themselves rather than worrying about living up to other people's expectations for their life

Learns to pick themselves back up again when falling

Weathers the storms to find the rainbows that make life beautiful

The Long Road Ahead

Packing her bags, she decides to leave home
She knows she's subjected herself to a lonely roam.
Somehow goodbye isn't that hard to say
Nothing would she trade to go back to the life of yesterday.

Every word and memory echoes in her mind
Now she hopes to be able to leave all that behind.
In places her heart is broken and fragile
An empty void left it partly dull.

They wanted her to be someone else by telling her lies
Faking a smile, her own reflection she failed to recognize.
Perfection in her they searched for
Not finding it, they had nothing to do with her anymore.

Constantly to strangers she was compared
What they really thought about her they openly shared.
Ridiculed and mocked, she got singled out
Every little flaw they talked about.

She tried to play it off as if nothing was wrong

Yet each night she cried herself to sleep,
thinking she didn't belong.
They crushed her spirit beneath their feet
Letting her know their expectations she failed
to meet.

Nothing she did was ever quite good enough
Hiding emotions, she learned how to be tough.
From the pain she wondered when she'd be
free
Till one day she left, discarding a past that had
become dreary.

As she looks back, she knows she's making the
right decision
To make things happen, she has to take action.
She doesn't even bother to ask why
For she all ready knows the truth they'll deny.

It's time for her to start over again
This life doesn't have to be the same as it was
back then.
In some areas her heart is still scarred
But rebuilding from the wreckage, she won't
watch what's left become charred.

Despite a rough past, in new beginnings she
allows herself to believe
Stepping forward, to the old ways she refuses
to cleave.
No one can take away the freedom she's fought
for
What matters is not what she's leaving behind
but what lies before.

For a reason she's been given a second chance
The possibilities in her life she's ready to enhance.
Upon a new path she begins to tread
Seeing beyond, she travels the long road ahead.

Second To None

Together forever is the promise you made
Never did I expect that for someone else me you'd trade.
I thought what we had was real
For you to use me and find someone else was never the deal.

If you didn't want to be with me you should have said so from the start
It would have prevented a broken heart.
Myself I blame for believing your lies
This game I should have learned sooner to recognize.

Did you honestly think you could have your cake and eat it too
Well with all your drama I'm through.
Second best I'm not going to be
I know the worth I have that you can't see.

Maybe to you I wasn't quite good enough
But one day you're going to see that without me it's tough.
It's not my fault you don't know a good thing even when it's gone
Guess you're too busy trying to find your next pawn.

I have too much respect for myself than being the one on the side
Without you a better life for me I can provide.
In your mind, I'm excess baggage you threw away
Yet my view is you didn't have what it took to stay.

Over wasted time no tears will I shed
New opportunities in my future wait ahead.
Your own path in life you chose
Now this chapter is just another I have to close.

I know I'll be all right
Because for what I want I always fight.
In time you will be nothing more than a distant memory
The scars you left behind I'll turn into marks of beauty.

So you turned to someone else in your time of need
That's okay myself through life I've always carried.
It's just too bad you couldn't see who you had in front of you
Sacrificing one for the other you knew you were going to do.

My self-esteem you can't break
Lucky for me, I learn from each mistake.
On me your words no longer have effect
Thanks to you, my heart I now fiercely protect.

Self-confidence I gained back
Moving forward, I won't backtrack.
I changed into a new person
Next time love comes my way, I'll be second to none.

What Words Can't Say

Behind those eyes lies an untold story
Inside beats a heart yearning to be free.
The invisible scars go unrevealed
So many hidden secrets remain concealed.

Out here it's easy to blend in with the background
No one notices you if you don't make a sound.
Better at times to keep quiet
Rather than say or do something that will cause a riot.

A silent spectator, you witness the violent scene
When did love become so brutal and mean?
Home is anywhere but a safe place to go
Too many things happen that people will never know.

By the memories your heart is stained
Smiling, that everything is okay you feigned.
Pain takes over as the truth burns inside
For only so long this tale of horror can you hide.

You know it's time for silence to be shattered
Yet people tend to look down on those who have been battered.

Thus you're faced with a challenging choice
Stay put or break free and use your voice.

They don't know how it is since in your place they never had to stand
You're not to blame for your past not going how you planned.
Caught in a deadly game, you had no say
All that matters is you made it out okay.

People pretend to know how you feel
But they weren't forced to participate in nightmares that turned real.
They tell you to move on and leave it all behind
If only they knew the battles fought when yourself you try to find.

The emotions locked up are so intense
Protecting a fragile heart, you build a fence.
Betrayed by ones you counted on, you don't know who to trust
Into a complex whirlwind of thoughts and feelings you get thrust.

Everyday is a fight just to survive
Facing the storms, you hope you come out alive.
A brief glimpse of your experiences words barely create
Unless they'd been there, one can't begin to imagine the depth of the hate.

All you can do is allow yourself to heal

Because no one else will ever really understand the pain you feel.
How can you make people see the past events of yesterday
When there's so much words aren't adequately able to say?

This Time Around

This hasn't exactly been the life I bargained for
But when one door closes somewhere opens another door.
I've learned that sometimes everything you have to lose
In order to see the path in life you should really choose.

Once trapped in darkness I couldn't see the light
With torn and bruised wings I wasn't ready to take flight.
A way out I tried to find
Hoping the pain forever I could leave behind.

For me no one ever fought
Between a painful past and a promising future I was caught.
Yet no one told me things weren't my fault
So guilt washed over me from each assault.

My heart only knew feelings of shame
Invisible to the world, I was just someone without a name.
A false act I put on
Not wanting anyone to suspect a part of me was gone.

Everyday the empty void inside continued to grow
Until the person I started to become I didn't know.
On this stage I stood, reciting lines that weren't mine
Words claiming everything was fine.

In different directions I got pulled
Smiling, into thinking nothing bothered me people I fooled.
Still, I felt like a puppet on a string forced to entertain
My own emotions I wasn't given a chance to explain.

People didn't want to hear what I had to say
Selfishly they expected me to be there to make them feel okay.
Forget the bad days I had
All I heard was I should be happy instead of sad.

Eventually things in my life began to fade
Pain for freedom I wanted to trade.
Screaming within, my cries went unheard
Because for someone positive to be sad seemed totally absurd.

Closer to the edge I found myself falling apart
There didn't seem to be much left to this broken heart.
So far away nothing felt real
I wondered if the wounds would ever heal.

Numbness took over me
Only one escape did I see.
The wrong alternative, my life I attempted to end
Unknowingly to me, up to heaven an SOS I did send.

Darkness engulfed me as I lost my grip
But now wasn't the time for me to make that last trip.
Intervening, God gave me back my breath
Saving me from this suicidal death.

Bits and pieces of my life flashed before my eyes
Finally I saw the truth buried beneath years of lies.
I wasn't some worthless, forgotten soul
A beautiful survivor, God granted me another chance to play the right role.

I've learned not to take my life for granted
I'll continue to grow and bloom where planted.
Some gray areas this life may hold
But waiting to be discovered, beauty stands ready to unfold.

Who I was yesterday is not who I am today
Fighting for my dreams, my courage and strength I'll quietly display.
My story is not near the end yet
I'm just now writing in the new changes I've met.

I won't forget where I came from but I won't let the past destroy me
It's the promise of a better future I now see.
My life is a miracle in every single way
This time around I'm going to make the most out of it as I live to the fullest each day.

Somewhere Tonight

Somewhere tonight lonely hearts cry out
Whether they should go on in life they're in doubt.
With each breath they take, their heart breaks more
In their own homes they're quickly becoming a casualty of a violent war.

Their battle wounds run very deep
At night, fearing for their safety, they don't even sleep.
A place of safety transforms into one where they're endangered
Into a deadly, vicious game they get lured.

The light in their eyes has gone out
Replaced by an expression of fear and doubt.
Behind closed doors a different story begins to unravel
A nightmarish hell in which alone they travel.

All traces of happiness have disappeared
Holding emotions back, their eyes haven't even teared.
Vacant looks stare out into the lonely night
Tired from long battles, they're exhausted from the fight.

Will the pain ever subside
Or will the hidden secrets they be forced to hide?
This isn't the movies where a hero comes to the rescue
Now it's about making the right choice on what to next do.

Drowning in a sea of loneliness, the current begins to pull them under
The reality is their life is one filled with unknown horror.
Yet the untold events trap them in silence
To unburden their story on someone else they feel would be a hindrance.

Falling, they try to rise to their feet
Weak from the emotional wounds, they feel beat.
Where are friends when they need them the most
Fading from existence they become a shadowy ghost.

Somewhere tonight someone is in need of a friend
Needing to talk so the pain inside can finally end.
They just want a chance to be heard
Before their life completely spirals downward.

A reason they look for to keep holding on
Salvaging what's left of their heart before it's

gone.
Assurance that they're not alone is what they need to hear
For then they'll know hope once again is near.
Somewhere tonight hurting is someone you know
Compassion and care to them will you show?
Now is the time they can use a friend on which to lean
Be the one there for them while the past and future they fight between.

Now or Never

In a peaceful, quiet place tonight I reside
It is here in this solitude I find hope and faith abide.
Looking up at the stars, I'm taken back to a time long ago
How different the life I had is compared to the one I now know.

Many times I traveled down heartache lane
Watching every dream I held end in vain.
Silence worked against me, becoming my public enemy
Losing myself, I had no idea who I even wanted to be.

The scars on my skin were nothing compared to the ones on my heart
Running deep, they got left behind by memories that tore it apart.
Things I saw and pain I felt I couldn't begin to describe
All I wondered was if anything for a broken heart anyone could prescribe.

Home turned into a word unknown and foreign
Ravaged by violence became the house in which I awoken.

Always staying on the outside I never knew love
For it was a feeling non-existent that to the side my family would shove.
No real happiness there could ever be found
How can any emotion survive where hate and violence abound?
The lesson I learned was how to fight so myself I'd be able to defend
In the outside world, that nothing happened I had to force myself to pretend.

Although the bruises long since faded, the emotional wounds remain
Those haunting memories of yesterday upon my heart managed to leave a stain.
Some days I still feel like the little girl in the corner clutching her teddy bear
Wishing I could run away to a safe refuge far away somewhere.

These fears though I have to fight off and defeat
Into the darkness of silence I cannot again retreat.
Yet part of me is fragile, alone, and very much afraid
Because major roles abandonment, betrayal and abuse in my life have played.

At times I hold back, not knowing how to express my innermost thoughts
They seem to be tied up in a million knots.
Speaking out is a battle in itself when other

survivors bully and judge
From their own hurtful pasts they continue to hold a grudge.

Standing here tonight, myself I really want to find
Every negative feeling of doubt I want to leave behind.
I yearn to know this life I've never known before
Within me, I believe there's something more.

I don't want the hurt and pain to prevail
Getting off this road leading to more heartbreak, I'm ready to travel a new trail.
No longer will I be afraid to let myself live
I refuse to allow my past to keep me captive.

A second chance with open arms I receive
Who cares what others think when what matters most is how myself I perceive.
Sometimes goodbye is a sign of real strength and courage
Letting go helps to break the bondage.

Gazing into the distance, I may not know yet what the future holds for me
But if I don't venture out, beyond the horizon I'll never see.
As I take a leap of faith, I know it's now or never
Cutting ties with the past, I say hello to my future.

Tears From Heaven

You saw her standing there today
Not saying anything, you chose to turn away.
Maybe you thought it wasn't your place to intervene
Clearly, though, all the evidence and proof on her face could be seen.

The chance to speak up you let pass by
Instead of saving a life, you helped sentence one to die.
A deaf ear you turned to the desperate cries
What you decided to believe was society's lies.

Too self absorbed in your own life, you pretended not to see
If only you'd taken the time, another innocent life wouldn't have had to pay the fee.
Playing it safe, from the situation you backed out
You allowed others to influence your doubt.

Rejecting her, you sent her back to that abusive hell
Now her story she'll never have a chance to tell.
In her time of need you left her all alone
But she ran out of strength to fight this battle on her own.

You were just far more important
Even though you knew what was going on,
you remained silent.
To you everything in your life was worth more
So while you lived in denial, she lay on the
floor, beaten and sore.

Another statistic she became
Because you refused to come forth and rescue
her from an evil game.
Her life she can never get back
At least she's in a better place, free from each
daily attack.

Tell me, does her face haunt you at night
Do you see in your dreams the girl for who
you wouldn't fight?
Does the guilt eat away at your conscience
Knowing you played an accomplice to her
absence.

Far away tonight this beautiful angel has flown
All she wanted was a little love and
compassion to be shown.
Her life didn't have to tragically end
It could have been different had someone
helped her broken heart mend.

Yet to brutal violence another soul was lost
No one wanted to speak on her behalf for fear
of the cost.
Silence took away her last breath
Firing the trigger that resulted in her death.

Forgotten and forsaken, she now watches from above
Wondering why no one would show her love.
From up there she hears the abused victims' every heart wrenching call
For them and the pain they feel her tears from heaven fall.

What If Tomorrow

You look at us and tell us we should smile
Yet you have no idea what it's like to live in exile.
For granted your life you take
But you can't begin to imagine others' heartache.

Inside your comfort zone you dwell
Boasting about how much you always excel.
That life is easy is the thought crossing your mind
Because you've never been the one left behind.

It's easy for you to say life isn't hard
By traumatic events you weren't scarred.
Yet us survivors you look down on
Not understanding why sometimes we are withdrawn.

You can't possibly know what it's like unless you've been there
Words will never really convey the real nightmare.
Sure to you easy life may appear
How would you feel though if everyday you lived in fear?

What if tomorrow you woke up to find your

life had changed
That nothing was the way you had it arranged.
Suddenly you find yourself having to fight to survive
Wondering if you'll even make it out alive.

What if tomorrow you played the victim role
Trapped without a voice, over your life you don't have control.
People pass you, not hearing your cries
Each night in bed you pray you'll see sunrise.

What if tomorrow you couldn't recognize the person staring back
All you saw were bruises from the previous night's attack.
Hiding behind a closed door, you're afraid to come out
As you lose yourself, you question what your life is about.

What if you sat on the other side
The pain so intense that part of you has died.
Ones who should love you are the ones who hurt you
Unable to speak out, no one comes to your rescue.

What if you found yourself all alone
Forgotten and forsaken, the trials you face on your own.
Into a dark sea of depression you plunge
How to escape becomes your greatest challenge.

What if tomorrow everyone you knew walked away
They decided they're too busy to help you get through the day.
Trust issues begin to abound
In your mind insecurities resound.

In a moment you can lose the life you held dear
The smile gives way to more than one tear.
You might think it could never happen to you
But it doesn't take long for things to completely change from what you knew.

Not to take our lives for granted we survivors learned
Our way through life we earned.
We only ask that our stories be heard
Because we fought hard for our pasts to be conquered.

Maybe compared to us your life seems so good
But you haven't stood where we once stood.
What if tomorrow your whole life changed
How would you handle it if people thought you were deranged?

Unexpected Fairytale

In a broken home she lives
One in which all her faults no one forgives.
Rejected and scorned, love is something she's never felt
Always running away, alone with her problems she's dealt.

She's the girl that nobody really sees
On her own this heavy burden she carries.
At night she cries herself to sleep
Wishing that her someone would want to keep.

Often because of her broken past she's dismissed
People don't want to be with her when they learn of what her life used to consist.
Without giving her a chance they say goodbye
Heartbroken again, she finds the words "I want to be with you" are a lie.

After awhile, with someone she ties the knot
But repeating her childhood, in the victim role she's caught.
So many tears he makes her cry
Driving her to the point she wishes she could die.

Her hopes and dreams he tears apart

Telling her from this marriage he wants to depart.
With nothing left to say, she watches him leave
The love she tried to give him he refused to receive.

Beneath her smiling mask her heart is bleeding and raw
The beauty in her he never even saw.
How he could throw her away she doesn't understand
This isn't the happily ever after she had planned.

Questioning what love is, this pain she doesn't want to feel
Suddenly nothing in her life seems real.
Emotionally abandoned, she closes the door on love
No longer believing she'll find the right one sent from above.

Sitting by the water, on paper she pours her emotions out
Trying to figure out what her life is now about.
A part of her longs for someone to save her from a painful past
Hoping maybe she can have that kind of love that forever does last.

Little does she know her knight in shining armor is waiting on the other side
That he's the one who will bring back to life the part of her that died.

One day out of the blue their paths by chance cross
He begins to help her piece things together among the chaos.
Past her scars he sees her real worth and value
Healing her heart, he's come to her rescue.
To him she's the most beautiful woman he's ever seen
Loving her for who she is of his heart she's queen.

At first this Cinderella wants to run away
Afraid it's all a dream that will fall apart and decay.
Holding her close, he looks deep into her eyes
The sincerity in his voice causes true feelings to rise.

For her he has chosen to fight
A future with her he wants to write.
He doesn't see her as someone broken and damaged
Just to have her in his life he feels privileged.

With honor and respect, he cherishes every moment together they spend
Soon she discovers herself falling in love with her best friend.
She wonders why she couldn't have met him sooner
What matters is he's here now, a part of her life's new chapter.

No longer holding back, on this journey of true

love she starts to embark
Believing in happily ever after again, between them she feels each spark.
Knowing it's meant to be, she doesn't run away or bail
For she knows she's finally found her unexpected fairytale.

Qualities That Make Survivors Stand Out

Ambition- we have that drive in us that keeps us going in life because we refuse to repeat our painful past

Beauty- people may just look at our emotional scars and physical scars, but underneath them lies so much beauty. It is our inner beauty that really shines through as our scars are just a testimony of what we survived and endured in our past.

Courage- breaking free in order to start our own lives and take back control takes a lot of courage on our part. We are courageous for taking that chance to break those chains and get out there on our own to find a better life for ourselves.

Determination- we look back and we see how we don't want our lives to be anymore. For too long we lived a life of pain that no one ever knew about. Now we are determined to rewrite our lives and begin new chapters to our life story.

Endurance- It takes endurance for us survivors

to rebuild our lives from the wreckage of the past. It's never easy to just start all over again after having been hurt and seen our lives along with all our dreams shattered apart. We have a strong will to pick up the pieces and begin to put them back together again as we allow ourselves to heal.

Fighting Spirit- We survivors have a fighting spirit in us and always have. If we did not have a fighting spirit then we would probably not be here today. The more we continue to fight for our rights and the rights of others, the more we can make this world a better place as we advance and go further in life.

Generosity- With survivors, it is in our nature to give back to others who have also been hurt in their own lives. When we give back, we're able to restore hope and faith to those who have lost it along the way. After all, helping our fellow survivors and victims is never about what we gain out of it; it's always about what we can give back and how we can save others from going through the same things we were forced to suffer through.

Helping Others- Because of what we went through, we know what it's like to go through the pain of abuse all alone and not having anyone to turn to. If it's one thing about us survivors, the one cause we are passionate about is stopping abuse in this world and letting the world know what goes on behind closed doors. We choose to help others so that they do not have to face things alone and so we can help prevent abuse from happening to future victims.

Insight- Survivors have more of an insight to another's situation because as survivors, we've been there before in our own lives. It is easier for someone who has gone through something similar to develop and have that insight over someone who hasn't ever experienced it. Therefore, as survivors, we are actually in a better position to really understand and see what other victims sand survivors have been through.

Kindness- Often when we hear of others going through the same things we did, our first instinct is to reach out a hand to them so they know they are not alone. It's the little acts of kindness that we do, the going above and beyond to really help others out that go a long way in life.

Love- Even though we may be cautious when it comes to love after being hurt, we also have it in us to show others what real love is and what unconditional love is like. It's always amazing to me how survivors who have been hurt in relationships, childhoods, or even in marriages still have all this love inside them that they are ready to give to others and give to that right person when they meet that right one who will treat them with respect and love them for who they are. Sometimes we are afraid to give into love but often when we find that right one, we're ready to take a chance on love. After all, we should be with someone who not only gives us that love we deserve but who receives the love that we have to offer.

Miracle of Us- I think we survivors are a miracle in ourselves. I say that because after everything we've been through, having gone through hell and back, and to be standing here today to share our stories is a miracle. We were the underdogs in life that no one expected to make it but yet here we are, having picked ourselves up and we didn't give up and they couldn't destroy our dreams. We are a miracle because we're proof that survivors can live through the pain and go on to have a better life free from the abuse.

New Beginnings- just because one chapter in our life has closed doesn't mean our life has ended. We still have a lot of living left to do and just because we went through hard times back then doesn't mean we will surrender and give up. Here we are fighting for what we believe in and here we are still holding onto our dreams to get those new beginnings in life. This is a brand new day and our future does not have to reflect our past in any way.

Open Mindedness- after living in silence for so long, without anyone hearing us, we are open minded to what others have been through without judging them for it. We know all too well what it's like to have others look down upon us and not take the time to get to know us for who we are or even see us for us. This is why we survivors tend to be respectful when it comes to what other survivors and victims have to say in telling their story. It is our open mind and our positive attitude that allows us to see beyond the horizons to where the endless possibilities lie.

Perseverance- When all around us everyone else wanted to give up, we continued to push ourselves in life. When they told us we wouldn't make it, we looked them in the eye and told them that yes we could and would make it. The ability to push ourselves even when we thought we couldn't last another mile in life is what has led us to our callings, purposes, and missions. Maybe people traveled the same road, but we decided to pave our own path in order to find out who we are and to see what our own lives hold for us.

Respect- Having broken free, we now carry ourselves with dignity, grace, and respect. Instead of tearing other survivors and victims down, we work together with them and show them the same respect that we want others to show us. After all, in order to gain respect from people, you must first show it. When we stop to help others, when we speak out, when we defend the truth, and when we stand for justice, it opens doors where people look up to us and seeing us in a new light, they begin to respect us for everything we went through.

Self-sacrifice- Survivors are some of the most selfless, self-sacrificing people there are, choosing to give of their time and themselves without expecting anything in return. Hard work and dedication on our part is what is helping to make these changes that we wish to see and helping to make a difference all over the world.

Thoughtful of Others- we tend to consider the needs of others and put them first probably because it's something we never had in our own lives. Left to fight alone, we had no one there who gave any thought to what we were facing. This is why we put so much thought into what others are feeling, we don't want them to feel alone and we want them to know there's always someone out there who cares and can relate.

Understanding- Why do survivors and victims come to us? They know we can relate to and understand them since we have been in that place in our lives before. People generally open up to those who they know have gone through some sort of similar experience in their own past. Sometimes it is easier to talk to someone who has been there, knowing they won't pass judgment but rather listen to us vent and pour our feelings out that have been locked up inside for a long time. We survivors understand each other because even though our situations and stories are all different, the one thing we do have in common is the pain we felt after enduring and surviving and coming out of it alive. We understand the struggles and the after effects since we fight them daily too. It is this common understanding that gives us survivors that special bond so to speak.

Vision- We survivors have this vision of what life can be without abuse and how the world can be if only the abuse in homes can be prevented and stopped. This vision is what drives us, motivates us and even inspires us to unite together to fight for the justice of all survivors and victims everywhere and to fight for their rights. It is our goal to ensure that no child grows up in a broken home, that no woman or man goes home to a spouse who beats them, that no one's innocence is stolen from them where they can't get those years back. We want people to enjoy life and not be afraid and live it in fear the way we did. So our vision is to stop all abuse so people may live in freedom.

Wisdom- the abuse we endured taught us many valuable lessons. From the lessons we learned from the past, we gained wisdom in knowing what not to do when it comes to our future, raising our own families, and even helping prepare the future generations to come. We can all learn from each other as well. If we put what we've learned together then we can educate those who don't know what the abuse is like. Together we can share our knowledge with the world to show the truth and grim realities of abuse.

Young At Heart- even though we were forced to grow up early, I think we survivors still remain young at heart because in a way, we're re discovering the youth we never had. I know for me, having grown up in a broken home where I couldn't enjoy my childhood, I'm kind of finding it again in the simple things life holds. I like being young at heart. As long as you know when to be serious and when to have fun in life and maintain that balance, then there is nothing wrong with being young at heart :). It's okay to get our part of our childhoods back that were lost long ago.

Zest- we definitely have zest for life. It's so much fun when we take chances and implement changes in our life to vary it up as we find the hidden beauty in life and as we take joy and pride in the little things from above that give it a whole new meaning. The zest we have gives us more of an appreciation for life as we soak it all up and make the most of what we have.

Attributes of Real Beauty That Make One Shine

Sadly in today's society, women and young girls have a lot of pressure placed on them for how they look physically. Many magazines tell them that they are not beautiful unless they are thin or look a certain way. No wonder so many women and young girls out there try hard to fit in and suffer from low self-esteems and struggle with eating disorders. They listen to society's lies and think they are not beautiful if they don't look like a super model. Even the media tries to destroy celebrities and point out their flaws as well; some of the celebrity women they've tried to say don't look good include Jessica Simpson, Jennifer Love Hewitt and Tyra Banks. But you know what, real beauty does not lie in the way that a person looks. A person is not beautiful because of how they look but they are beautiful because of how their heart is on the inside. Yet, the world seems to disregard inner beauty and only go by what they can see on the outside. Thus, they are blinded to the beauty underneath that really makes a person shine. Don't starve yourself or change yourself because of what society claims is in style and what's beautiful. Society is often shallow and it's their shallowness that is destroying the truly beautiful people out there. I think if people would take the time to really look inside a person's heart, they would discover all the beauty that is there. The following is a list of attributes I came up with that make someone truly beautiful and none of them include physical features since my theory is that when you are attracted to a person's personality then the person becomes attractive to you in every area.

These are the attributes of real beauty:

caring, kind and compassionate nature

loving heart

humble and meek spirit

positive attitude and outlook in life

contagious smile that brightens another's day

empathy and sympathy for others in the challenges and trials they face

keeping an open mind to things that the world views as different and unacceptable

understanding without passing judgment

lending a helping hand to those in need

courage to stand up for what's right

strength to rise above

being young at heart

seeing people for who they are without focusing on their flaws

determination and a strong will to make it in life without giving up

being able to laugh even through the hard times

surviving the storm in order to dance in the rain afterwards

speaking out for those who have no voice

fighting for the justice of others

showing and teaching what love is

embracing the possibilities life holds

believing in the power of dreams and pursuing them to make them come true

taking chances on doing new things in life that will lead to better places

slowing down to enjoy the small pleasures in

life rather than taking them for granted

reaching out and being a friend to those who find themselves alone in life

refusing to stoop down to the level of those who hurt us

setting a good example for those around us by being a good role model for others

learning lessons from the past and applying them to the future

picking ourselves up even after we fall down in life

being the architects of our lives by rebuilding from the wreckage and making from it what we want our lives to be

not letting little things get to us and not sweating the small stuff but rather focusing on the more important issues going on in the world that need care and attention

turning rejection into something positive by using it as our drive to get where we want to be

loving ourselves and accepting ourselves exactly the way we are

implementing changes in our lives when

things don't go the way we planned

building others up by encouraging them
instead of discouraging them by attacking
them and tearing into them
choosing to hear both sides of a story before
making assumptions about another's life

preventing rumors about someone and going
to the person they're about to get the truth

realizing that sometimes saying goodbye is not
a sign of weakness but a sign of strength when
we cut ties with negative influences in our lives
bringing us down

closing the chapters of our previous lives that
we left behind as we write a new beginning for
the life that is waiting for us now

offering constructive criticism and helpful
advice instead of destructive criticism that can
demolish a person's hope in life

encouraging people in their healing journey in
life instead of getting jealous of them when
they're out there doing good for others and
making something of their lives

using our talents to benefit others and giving
back to others through our talents without
seeking recognition and fame for the work we
do

creating an impact on others' lives by just being
ourselves

rebelling against society's rules and finding our
own path in life as we follow our hearts over
their dumb rules that are false

defying ignorance and exposing the truth
about how life really is, that it isn't easy and
never will be but that we are strong survivors
standing here today because of our hard work
to break free and move forward in our lives

helping to put back together the pieces of
broken hearts that have been shattered apart
from traumatic events

spreading hope and faith by sharing our stories
and talking about our own personal
experiences

seeing beyond the outer appearance of people
to see the beauty beneath the scars

taking the negative experiences in our lives
and turning them into something positive
which not only helps us but others around us
as well

helping others to their feet when they fall and
not leaving them behind

appreciating the little acts of kindness others
do for us and making sure to let them know

how much we appreciate them and are
thankful for them

telling those we love and care about how much
we love and care about them every single day

Road To Salvation

On a deserted street travels a lonely stranger tonight
Just trying to hold on to see the morning light.
Mile after mile keep rolling on
Yet still the past memories are not gone.

Out here only her thoughts accompany her on this journey
They serve to remind her why she wants so badly to be free.
Always running away, a place to call home she can't find
Being anywhere else is better than what she left behind.

That she's even missing no one is aware
Then again when she was around they didn't care.
The way others treated her she never felt she belonged
Remaining silent, not a word she spoke when her they wronged.

Trying to block out scenes from before, they replay in her mind
Haunting her every move, it's as if her own death warrant has been signed.
These things she can't talk about
Because her story people will just doubt.

Pain from hidden secrets burn inside
Most of her emotions long ago died.
The last time she knew happiness she's unable to recall
When life started to look up, something would cause her to fall.

With a broken heart she packs up what's left of her old life
Pieces scattered along the trail were torn apart by strife.
Here and there lay tiny fragments on the ground
Having fallen away from the past to which they were bound.

No friendly faces does she meet
Stress weighing down on her, she feels exhausted and beat.
If only she could find somewhere to rest
Maybe finally over would be this test.

Out here she's searching for something more
Hoping she'll be able to find an open door.
Though her faith falters, she wants a new start
As she tries to save what's left of her broken heart.

Far from everything she once knew she looks for better
It's time to destroy this scarlet letter.
Sinking to her knees, she begins to cry
She doesn't want her life to continue to pass her by.

This isn't how it should be
Negativity shouldn't be the only thing she can see.
Turning over a new leaf, she decides to go in a different direction
Looking for peace and forgiveness, she travels down the road to salvation.

When I Look At You

You look at yourself, not always seeing someone strong
With the past catching up, you wonder where you belong.
Many times you just want to run away
How you truly feel you aren't exactly sure what to say.

The walls seem to be closing in
Some days you feel that more battles you lose than win.
Old insecurities whisper in your ear
Every remark about how you were never good enough you hear.

Emotional scars have left your heart battered
Reminders that your self-esteem was long ago shattered.
Pieces of your life vanish before your eyes
A voice inside your head tells you so many lies.

Looking in the mirror, the glass you want to break
In your mind's perspective you think you're a mistake.
Your view only shows the flaws you see
Always trying to be perfect you had to pay a big fee.

Into a million pieces your broken heart begins to beat
Bravely on your own each challenge you meet.
Yet in your eyes you continue to fall short
Crashing around you come the walls of your fort.

Everything you don't see I can see in you
How beautiful you really are I only wish you knew.
Your characteristics and traits make you very unique
After surviving all you've been through, you're far from weak.

Gone is the scared person you used to be
Standing there now is a strong warrior who broke free.
I admire the strength in you that's helped you get far
To me you're a bright shining star.

I know you for the fighter you are
In my eyes your image nothing can mar.
Your inner beauty from within radiates
An amazing individual it creates.

The reflection I have doesn't show a vulnerable, fragile soul
Before me is someone growing and healing in the survivor role.
By who you are today you're defined
The past didn't ruin you because to it you weren't permanently assigned.

Venturing out, your own sequel you began to write
To do that means of your dreams you never lost sight.
So much courage it took to leave that life behind
That makes you a hero and champion in my mind.

You may not realize it but you are a positive role model
For other survivors you set a good example.
Life isn't easy yet you hold onto your hope
Fighting back when your back's against the rope.

Giving up was the decision you could have chose
From the ashes of your past though, you rose.
Now you search for something more
Taking chances to walk through a new door.

That you're not good enough never believe
Encouragement and inspiration from you people receive.
You're truly worth so much more than you know
When I look at you, how beautiful you are I wish to you I could show.

Ghost Town

A town once full of life, she doesn't recognize it anymore
Can this be the same place that was so alive before?
Now it lays empty and covered in dust
Abandoned buildings have begun to rust.

In the air hangs so much sorrow
Over the town depression casts a shadow.
At one time it held so much promise
Things were different when people were fearless.

She rummages through debris, wondering what's left to salvage
It's hard to believe such chaos could create all this damage.
Her mind takes her back to the way it used to be
When the atmosphere was happy and carefree.

Back then there wasn't anything to fear
One could establish safe residence here.
Families knew the meaning of love
Neighbors helped each other out when push came to shove.

Life was like heaven on earth
Hope and faith gave dreams birth.

No one expected it to fall apart
Because endless lay the possibilities to get a new start.
Soon, though, the life as she knew it came to an end
Somewhere along the way tragedy happened.
Against each other people turned
Betraying friends and family, one another they burned.

Through the streets violence swept
Into households danger crept.
Silence drowned out voices needing to be heard
With no help around, hurting hearts couldn't be cured.

The days of feeling safe vanished
Those who fought and spoke out were banished.
At war with each other, the town divided
As darkness took over, by their own pasts people were haunted.

Looking at the dilapidated houses and buildings reminds her of times she fell
When her own world shattered because she had no one to tell.
Every demon she battled alone
Having to find a way to survive when her the family decided to disown.

Just like this empty town, she felt hollow inside
For a while the pain in her heart she denied.

Under the pressure, she almost broke
But to the truth about who she really was she awoke.
Going through the remains of the wreckage, memories she recovers that were buried
Emotions surging through her are varied.
Once again she can sense the ghosts of yesterday's presence
Except this time they won't trap her in deathly silence.

This town she may not be able to rebuild
But with hope to build a better life her heart is filled.
Her life won't remain empty, abandoned, and forsaken like this ghost town
Creating a new life, she refuses to break down.

Nothing To Lose

I thought I had my life all figured out
When it came to my dreams I never had any doubt.
So many plans for myself I made
Then things changed and it all began to fade.

Into a world of chaos I was thrown
Where every trial and challenge I faced on my own.
My own family became strangers I didn't know
Forced to carry on alone, guidance they wouldn't show.

I never knew such pain my past could create
Breaking down inside, I wondered if this time I'd meet my fate.
Memories I held onto for so long
Feeling that somehow I was the one who did wrong.

Time and time again, I found myself running away
Pushing away people because I was afraid to stay.
Within me raged a battle very intense
Hurting from emotional wounds, I put up a wall of defense.

More than anything I wanted to go back and

make it all right
Instead the haunting demons I constantly had to fight.
From everything in my life I felt cut off and isolated
Pieces of my heart fell apart and separated.

I just wanted my life back
Yet I wandered along, struggling to find safety from each attack.
A sign or some kind of reassurance I looked for to tell me where to go
Because the girl I used to be I didn't know.

A stranger in my own life, I stood on the outside looking in
Wondering if these battles I could possibly win.
I didn't want to hurt anymore
My heart longed for the life I dreamed of before.

Over me I couldn't let the past have control
The demons from yesterday would not own my soul.
My perspective I needed to change
So that for myself a better life I could arrange.

Standing my ground, on my inner strength I learned to rely
I channeled my energy on living for now and not asking why.
In my mind this beautiful future I envisioned
For it to begin though I had to let my old life

end.

Now here I am, believing in myself more than ever
Possibilities are endless when from my vocab I remove the word never.
With no regrets to really live my life again I choose
Maybe I don't know what tomorrow brings, but I know I have nothing to lose.

When Night Falls

For too long I stayed here
Making any excuse not to face my fear.
This false charade I put on for the world to see
The more I denied anything was wrong, I became more unhappy.

Many sacrifices I made
Wishing this life of pain I could trade.
Every time I pushed things to the side, more of myself I'd lose
Because trying to be what you wanted is what I decided to choose.

Too busy living for you, my true self I abandoned
Telling myself it would change, your actions I pardoned.
Deep within, though, I knew nothing would ever be the same
From you I felt the resentment that into your life I even came.

For your approval and acceptance I secretly yearned
But every bridge to my dreams I built you only burned.
None of my efforts were really good enough
My attempts to make something of my life you found a way to rebuff.

My heart I trusted you to protect
Yet all emotions I felt you wrecked.
Knowing you wouldn't hear me, I remained silent
A fly on the wall in your life, you failed to notice I was absent.

I had to find out the hard way that from you no love I'd receive
Too busy tearing into me, never once in me did you believe.
A list of all my faults and mistakes you threw in my face
Letting me know to you I was just a disgrace.

If I stayed, my life would never get better
I'd never be able to rid myself of your scarlet letter.
Better to face my fears of being alone
So not one piece of me you could continue to own.

Defying your rules for my life, against you I rebelled
To your expectations no longer would I be held.
You tried to break me down once but to no avail
Finding out who I really am, the real me I'll finally unveil.

Freedom from this painful past is worth every bit the fight

Saying goodbye, a new part of my life I keep in sight.
Every horizon I want to explore
Because I'm tired of being caught in your war.

It's time for me to pack my bags, leaving the past behind
To your plans for me I refuse to be confined.
The chance to get out there and be myself I'll take
Walking away, I know when night falls, I won't be afraid to face daybreak.

Ticket To Freedom

A one-way ticket she holds in her hands
Waiting for the bus, with the other passengers she stands.
Surrounded by strangers, she feels out of place
This journey to freedom, though, on her own she must face.

The events leading up to this moment she never planned
Why they happened she still doesn't understand.
Like a fugitive driven from her home, she finds herself here
Feeling nervous and scared, nothing seems clear.

As she boards the bus, her heart pounds faster in her chest
That she'd be leaving home for good at 17 she wouldn't have guessed.
She knows it's better than the alternative
Because her painful past she doesn't want to relive.

Taking a seat, she stares out the window
For the first time her heart she finds a little hard to follow.
To go back would mean facing a life of emotional imprisonment

Those old demons she'd rather not confront.

Now the bus pulls out, leaving this town behind
So begins the journey in which herself she must find.
Mile after mile rolls on, taking her farther away
Alone with her thoughts, memories replay.

Though she's afraid, she's more afraid of returning to that place
Where every part of who she was they tried to erase.
Fear ruled the premises of a once happy household
Many dark secrets from within those walls remained untold.

She shivers, thinking about what she was reduced to
It's a miracle she survived the things she went through.
Leaning back, she wonders if her life she can make right
All she's ever known is to survive and fight.

The fear inside her she doesn't openly show
Where she is going now she doesn't really know.
Gaining her freedom was her choice
Just starting out, she has yet to discover the full power of her voice.

Right now she has no idea about the difference

she'll go on to make
But as time goes by she'll realize her life wasn't and isn't a mistake.
For this journey by the past she was being prepared
She lived so her story with others could be shared.

This bus ride is only the beginning to what her future holds
It won't be long before the true meaning of her life unfolds.
With one ticket her life she got to reclaim
Looking ahead and not back, it will never be the same.

Smiling Through the Tears

To you she's another friendly face you pass on the street
Someone who for a brief moment you happen to meet.
Exchanging greetings you go your own way
Never once do you think about the stranger you saw earlier that day.

She walks on, disappearing out of sight
Ready to take on yet another day in her life's fight.
So much she holds back, refusing to show her other side
Some secrets are just better to hide.

A regular life is what she wants to lead
One where past memories are forever buried.
Still she struggles with being able to completely let go
Confused, she's not sure which path to follow.

There's never been anyone to give her guidance
Losing herself, the girl she used to be and the one she is now bear no resemblance.
From everyone else she remains distant
Not knowing how to let them in, she puts up a front.

For a long time as someone else she's tried to masquerade
Denying anything is wrong, she plays out her own charade.
Left with a sense of longing, this unknown feeling she can't name
The shattered pieces of her bruised heart leave her with guilt and shame.

In her own life she's been the hero
Always pulling herself up so she wouldn't fall below.
Being the strong one, herself she thought she could save
Parts of her though a haunting past continues to enslave.

People only see the side she chooses to reveal
Looking at her tough side, they think she's made of steel.
Of her true self she feels like a cardboard cut out
Her sunny demeanor doesn't tell others what she's really about.

She wonders how she's managed to survive this long
When everything in her life has seemed to go wrong.
What she wouldn't give just to feel alive again
To forget the pain she suffered back then.

Missing pieces of her heart she wants to complete

In order to have a foundation to stand on that's concrete.
Who she really is she longs to know
No more does she want to be her own foe.

You never see past the faces you pass every day
Many hide the fact that they're losing their way.
Inside they cry out, hoping from a life of pain they can be liberated
Searching for a lifeline, smiling through the tears, they conceal a heart wounded.

Building New Bridges

Upon the rocky waves of life's storms we've been tossed
Far from shore we find ourselves quickly becoming lost.
Rain pours down, dampening our spirits and blocking out the sun
As the sky darkens, from our view fades the horizon.

Trying to fight the current, we start to sink below
Our strength weakens as back to safety we attempt to row.
The challenging winds carry us even farther away
Soon the memories of our lives right before our eyes replay.

So many events flash through our mind
If we leave here, what kind of life will we be leaving behind?
We see chances we had that we discarded
Friends and family we pushed aside because ourselves we doubted.

There were moments our hearts got crushed
When to the side our hopes and dreams were brushed.
Our lives by the very people we trusted to be

there were abandoned
Betraying us, new wounds they opened.

Wrapped up in our pain, we became more distant and reserved
Blinded to the signs, off the road we swerved.
A roadblock we crashed right into
Not knowing if this collision we'd survive through.

Pieces of our hearts seemed to separate
We wondered if this life of pain was our fate.
For a long time we stayed stuck in one place
Everything we once knew vanished without a trace.

Now as we battle the storm, we realize where we went wrong
How numbed with grief into a world of isolation we plunged headlong.
Is this the way our story will end
Or the continuation of a new beginning can we extend?

Maybe we had a rough start but it's not too late to turn things around
To a painful past we don't have to be bound.
Dark times won't always last
Fighting them off, our lives can have a sunny and positive forecast.

Strength surges through us as we rise above the surface
In knowing we survived the storm we find

solace.
The sun breaks out, revealing the long sought for shore
Our hope it begins to restore.

The past we can't go back and undo
But a different path we can follow as we make a breakthrough.
Many old bridges we'll have to burn
Building new bridges, to a new day we return.

About The Author

Jenna Kandyce Linch is a child abuse and domestic violence survivor who uses her writing to reach out and encourage others who are healing from abuse. Many of her poems reflect things from her own childhood and former marriage. Currently she resides in Florida where she is working on a petition for government-funded schools established for victims and survivors of abuse to go to learn how to heal and deal with issues they have been through. To find out more about Linch, you can visit her personal site at www.myspace.com/survivorinlife and you can also find out more about the petition for Hope For Healing Hearts at www.myspace.com/schoolsforsurvivors.

www.ingramcontent.com/pod-product-compliance
Lightning Source LLC
Chambersburg PA
CBHW031613160426
43196CB00006B/117